Living Liturgy™

for Extraordinary Ministers of Holy Communion

Living Liturgy™

for Extraordinary Ministers of Holy Communion

Year A • 2008

Joyce Ann Zimmerman, C.PP.S.
Thomas A. Greisen
Kathleen Harmon, S.N.D. de N.
Thomas L. Leclerc, M.S.

LITURGICAL PRESS
Collegeville, Minnesota

www.litpress.org

Design by Ann Blattner. Art by Annika Nelson.

Excerpts from the *Lectionary for Mass for Use in the Dioceses of the United States* copyright © 1970, 1986, 1997, 1998, 2001 Confraternity of Christian Doctrine, Inc., Washington, D.C. All rights reserved. No part of this work may be reproduced or transmitted in any form or by any means, electronic or mechanical, including photocopying, recording, or by any information storage and retrieval system, without permission in writing from the copyright holder.

© 2007 by Order of Saint Benedict, Collegeville, Minnesota. All rights reserved. No part of this book may be reproduced in any form, by print, microfilm, microfiche, mechanical recording, photocopying, translation, or by any other means, known or yet unknown, for any purpose except brief quotations in reviews, without the previous written permission of Liturgical Press, Saint John's Abbey, P.O. Box 7500, Collegeville, Minnesota 56321-7500. Printed in the United States of America.

ISSN 1933-3129

ISBN 13: 978-0-8146-3084-6

Presented to

_____

*in grateful appreciation
for ministering as an
Extraordinary Minister
of
Holy Communion*

_____

_____
(date)

USING THIS RESOURCE

By baptism we are all made members of the Body of Christ. Extraordinary ministers of Holy Communion, then, minister the Body and Blood of Christ to the Body of Christ. They visibly nourish and strengthen the Body of Christ. Rather than having any kind of extra "status" in the liturgical community, these ministers are servants of the servants, as Jesus himself showed us at the Last Supper. They are called "extraordinary" not because of any personal worthiness or honor but because the "ordinary" ministers of Holy Communion are the bishops, priests, deacons, or instituted acolytes. In the typical parish situation, however, large numbers of the faithful come forward for Communion, and so in most cases lay members of the parish are designated as "extraordinary" ministers so that the Communion procession does not become disproportionately long.

Preparing for this ministry

As with all ministry, extraordinary ministers of Holy Communion must prepare themselves for their ministry if it is to mean more than simply getting a job done. This book is intended, first, to be a guide and resource for preparing to minister and, second, to be a help for these ministers to deepen their eucharistic spirituality. Each Sunday and some key feast days of the liturgical year include the gospel text (or a shortened version of it), prayer, and reflection suggestions. The use of the first person plural (we, us) of the text implies a group is present for the preparation; these texts are conveniently worded for when two or more extraordinary ministers gather for preparation, or when these texts are used in the context of the rite of Holy Communion with the homebound and sick.

Holy Communion for the sick

Jesus' preaching of the Good News in the gospel is made visible by his many and varied good works on behalf of others. Perhaps more than any other group, Jesus reaches out with his healing touch to those who are sick, and this compassionate ministry continues today in the life of the church. One of the many blessings of parishes who have extraordinary ministers of Holy Communion is that parishioners who are sick or homebound or those in hospitals and other institutions can share in the liturgical life of the parish more frequently. Extraordinary ministers are reminded that the sick and suffering share in a special way in Jesus' passion. The ministers can bring hope and consolation and the strength of the Bread of Life to those who seem cut off from active participation in parish life.

Adapting this resource for Holy Communion for the sick
It is presumed that each Communion minister is familiar with the rites for Communion with the sick. There is a brief rite for those in hospitals or other institutions; this shorter rite is used when the circumstances would not permit the longer rite. The longer rite is used in ordinary circumstances and includes a Liturgy of the Word preceding the Communion rite. When using the longer rite, the opening and closing prayer of this book would nicely round out the beginning and end of the service; the gospel is conveniently included to proclaim the word, and a reflection might be shared.

Privilege and dignity
It is indeed a unique privilege to serve members of the parish as extraordinary ministers of Holy Communion, both at the parish Masses and by bringing Communion to the sick and homebound. The parish's presence through the minister to the sick and homebound is a particular sign of their dignity as members of the Body of Christ. The Communion minister is in a unique position to bring hope and comfort to those who may find little in life to comfort them. May this ministry always be a sign of Jesus' great love and compassion for all his Father's beloved daughters and sons!

FIRST SUNDAY OF ADVENT

The gospel for this First Sunday of Advent invites us to prepare for the coming of the Son of Man at the end of time. Let us ready ourselves to encounter him as he comes to us now in the many circumstances of our lives . . .

Prayer

Gracious God, you come to us at unexpected times and in surprising ways. As we begin Advent, help us to open ourselves to your presence and welcome you with sincere hearts. We ask this through Christ our Lord. **Amen.**

Gospel (Matt 24:37-44)

Jesus said to his disciples: "As it was in the days of Noah, so it will be at the coming of the Son of Man. In those days before the flood, they were eating and drinking, marrying and giving in marriage, up to the day that Noah entered the ark. They did not know until the flood came and carried them all away. So will it be also at the coming of the Son of Man. Two men will be out in the field; one will be taken, and one will be left. Two women will be grinding at the mill; one will be taken, and one will be left. Therefore, stay awake! For you do not know on which day your Lord will come. Be sure of this: if the master of the house had known the hour of night when the thief was coming, he would have stayed awake and not let his house be broken into. So too, you also must be prepared, for at an hour you do not expect, the Son of Man will come."

Brief Silence

For Reflection

We largely remain oblivious to the deeper movement within us of the unfolding of time, unaware that in the midst of daily, mundane activities—like eating, drinking, marrying, grinding at the mill, etc.—God's work of salvation is drawing nearer. Thus, time is not a "container" of mundane events, but is advancing toward something *new*—Christ's definitive coming and the fullness of salvation.

Would we live differently today if we did not believe Jesus is coming? Our belief in this compels us to "stay awake" by conforming our lives *now* into the ways of the kingdom *coming*. "Stay awake" is not to be taken literally. No, we do not know when "the Son of Man" will come again or how God's kingdom will be established—whether peaceably or by destruction. Yet the readings and Advent call us to look forward to the future with hope and expectation. Why? Because Christ's Second Coming will bring to completion God's work of salvation.

✦ I understand Jesus' command "Stay awake" to mean . . . I am growing in my preparedness for when "the Son of Man will come" by . . .

Brief Silence

Prayer

O God, you will come in the fullness of time to gather all back into your loving arms. Help us to live now the love you always extend us in the Eucharist and to love all those we meet. We ask this through Christ our Lord. **Amen.**

THE IMMACULATE CONCEPTION OF THE BLESSED VIRGIN MARY

On this solemnity of the Immaculate Conception, we look to Mary's holiness as a model for our own living. Let us reflect on our actions this week and examine how faithful we have been to our baptismal call to holiness . . .

Prayer

Almighty God, you prepared Mary to be the mother of your divine Son, preserving her free from sin from the very moment of her conception. Help us, through the intercession of the Blessed Virgin Mary, to resist sin and be faithful always to your holy will. We ask this through Christ our Lord. **Amen**.

Gospel **(Luke 1:26-38)**

The angel Gabriel was sent from God to a town of Galilee called Nazareth, to a virgin betrothed to a man named Joseph, of the house of David, and the virgin's name was Mary. And coming to her, he said, "Hail, full of grace! The Lord is with you." But she was greatly troubled at what was said and pondered what sort of greeting this might be. Then the angel said to her, "Do not be afraid, Mary, for you have found favor with God. Behold, you will conceive in your womb and bear a son, and you shall name him Jesus. He will be great and will be called Son of the Most High, and the Lord God will give him the throne of David his father, and he will rule over the house of Jacob forever, and of his Kingdom there will be no end." But Mary said to the angel, "How can this be, since I have no relations with a man?" And the angel said to her in reply, "The Holy Spirit will come upon you, and the power of the Most High will overshadow you. Therefore the child to be born will be called holy, the Son of God. And behold, Elizabeth, your relative, has also conceived a son in her old age, and this is the sixth month for her who was called barren; for nothing will be impossible for God." Mary said, "Behold, I am the handmaid of the Lord. May it be done to me according to your word." Then the angel departed from her.

Brief Silence

For Reflection

What reaction might *we* have if we heard an angel say to *us*, "Hail, full of grace, the Lord is with you"? In fact, this is exactly what is promised to us in baptism. Mary "found favor with God." What does this mean for us? Just as both Mary and her divine Son said yes to God's will for them, so are we called through our baptismal commitment to do the same. Like Mary, our whole lives are to be spent hearing God's word and saying yes to God's will. True, Mary and Jesus were conceived in privileged moments. But that doesn't mean that their example of holiness and fidelity is beyond us. Their lives were ordinary—wife and mother, son of a carpenter—but they lived the ordinary "according to [God's] word." Our ordinary days—being wife or husband, mother or father, brother or sister, neighbor or friend, employer or employee—are to be lived as a yes to God. This is how we are holy too.

Holiness, then, means simply living so that others encounter God's presence within us. We don't need to do anything "extra" to be holy; we simply need to do the everyday things with the conviction that we are God's adopted sons and daughters, called to say yes to God's will. By keeping God's presence ever before us, we can be that presence for others.

✦ What helps me recall that God dwells within me is . . . I am God's presence for others whenever I . . .

Brief Silence

Prayer

Loving God, you give us the grace of your very life. Help us to be faithful to whatever you ask of us, so that we may be holy in your eyes. We ask this through Christ our Lord. **Amen.**

SECOND SUNDAY OF ADVENT

John the Baptist prepared for the coming of Christ by calling the people to repentance. Let us prepare for Christ's coming and for celebrating Eucharist by turning from sin and asking for God's mercy . . .

Prayer

Lord God our Father, you prepared for our salvation from the beginning of time. Help us to hear John the Baptist's message to repent and to live faithfully our baptismal commitment. We ask this through Christ our Lord. **Amen.**

Gospel (Matt 3:1-12)

John the Baptist appeared, preaching in the desert of Judea and saying, "Repent, for the kingdom of heaven is at hand!" It was of him that the prophet Isaiah had spoken when he said: / *A voice of one crying out in the desert, / Prepare the way of the Lord, / make straight his paths.* / John wore clothing made of camel's hair and had a leather belt around his waist. His food was locusts and wild honey. At that time Jerusalem, all Judea, and the whole region around the Jordan were going out to him and were being baptized by him in the Jordan River as they acknowledged their sins.

When he saw many of the Pharisees and Sadducees coming to his baptism, he said to them, "You brood of vipers! Who warned you to flee from the coming wrath? Produce good fruit as evidence of your repentance. And do not presume to say to yourselves, 'We have Abraham as our father.' For I tell you, God can raise up children to Abraham from these stones. Even now the ax lies at the root of the trees. Therefore every tree that does not bear good fruit will be cut down and thrown into the fire. I am baptizing you with water, for repentance, but the one who is coming after me is mightier than I. I am not worthy to carry his sandals. He will baptize you with the Holy Spirit and fire. His winnowing fan is in his hand. He will clear his threshing floor and gather his wheat into his barn, but the chaff he will burn with unquenchable fire."

Brief Silence

For Reflection

John, anticipating the judgment Christ's coming would bring, prepared "the way of the Lord" by calling the people to repentance. We heed John's message by converting our way of living and bearing good fruit. John baptized with water; followers of Jesus are baptized with "the Holy Spirit and fire." The image of fire reminds us that we are purified and made holy by our baptism; we receive the Holy Spirit and God's life is within us. This is what empowers us to bear fruit. All we need do is say yes to God's will and be faithful to our baptismal call. We also remember that baptism plunges us into Christ's dying and rising. Conforming ourselves to Christ, we are challenged to die to self for the sake of others.

This is a time of the year when many opportunities to think of others arise. The red kettle and bell ringing remind us that others are less fortunate than we are and need our help. At the same time, we cannot forget to be mindful of those with whom we live, work, and play, especially at a time when busyness might cause us to be tired and short-tempered and when getting our own things taken care of might cause us to be so shortsighted that we do not see the need of those close to us.

✦ If John were here today the challenge he would place upon me is . . . As an extraordinary minister of Holy Communion, this means to me . . .

Brief Silence

Prayer

O God, you feed us with the Bread of Life. Help us to be faithful to the grace you have given us and to repent of all that keeps us from more perfectly loving you and others. We ask this through Christ our Lord. **Amen.**

THIRD SUNDAY OF ADVENT

In this Sunday's gospel Jesus reveals himself as the promised Savior who comes to heal and save. As we prepare to celebrate Christmas, let us ask Jesus to heal and save us . . .

Prayer

Loving and healing God, you care for the needs of each of us by sending your Son to announce the Good News of salvation. Help us to recognize Jesus in our midst and to be as open to him as was John the Baptist. We ask this through Christ our Lord. **Amen.**

Gospel (Matt 11:2-11)

When John the Baptist heard in prison of the works of the Christ, he sent his disciples to Jesus with this question, "Are you the one who is to come, or should we look for another?" Jesus said to them in reply, "Go and tell John what you hear and see: the blind regain their sight, the lame walk, lepers are cleansed, the deaf hear, the dead are raised, and the poor have the good news proclaimed to them. And blessed is the one who takes no offense at me."

As they were going off, Jesus began to speak to the crowds about John, "What did you go out to the desert to see? A reed swayed by the wind? Then what did you go out to see? Someone dressed in fine clothing? Those who wear fine clothing are in royal palaces. Then why did you go out? To see a prophet? Yes, I tell you, and more than a prophet. This is the one about whom it is written: / *Behold, I am sending my messenger ahead of you; / he will prepare your way before you.* / Amen, I say to you, among those born of women there has been none greater than John the Baptist; yet the least in the kingdom of heaven is greater than he."

Brief Silence

For Reflection

This Sunday's gospel tells us that John is in prison. "Is this what it all comes to?" we might well imagine John asking himself. Instead, John asks a very different question. From the dark of prison and on the brink of death, John asks an urgent question: "Are you the one . . . or should we look for another?" Jesus honors the question by providing an answer; moreover, his answer is specific and concrete: "the blind regain their sight, the lame walk, lepers are cleansed, the deaf hear, the dead are raised, and the poor have the good news proclaimed to them."

John's question must become our own: Is Jesus the One for us, or are we really looking for another? In trying to answer the question of Jesus' identity, we cannot rely only on the authority of others found in creeds or catechisms. Our answer must also come from our own personal experience of Jesus and the good fruit of his life and ministry. Advent is a time when we can open our eyes to see in new ways the presence of Jesus—in good actions, in the holiness of others, in forgiveness and healing. Yes, we see Jesus when we see the fruits of his presence.

✦ The works that I have heard and seen that make me believe Jesus is the Messiah are . . . My own expectations of who Jesus is have blinded me to his advent when . . .

Brief Silence

Prayer

O God, you are both far and near. Be with us as we prepare for Christmas, nourish us with Holy Communion so that we can see your presence among us, and help us to be faithful in proclaiming the Gospel by the goodness of our lives. We ask this through Christ our Lord. **Amen.**

FOURTH SUNDAY OF ADVENT

Joseph believed and obeyed the God who spoke to him in a dream. Let us open our hearts to God's speaking to us in our ordinary lives and reflect on how God is made present to us in our daily living . . .

Prayer

Awesome God, you sent your divine Son to be Emmanuel, God is with us. Be with us as we anticipate our Christmas celebration, that we might be faithful to being disciples of Jesus and make known his presence and gift of salvation. We ask this through Christ our Lord. **Amen.**

Gospel (Matt 1:18-24)

This is how the birth of Jesus Christ came about. When his mother Mary was betrothed to Joseph, but before they lived together, she was found with child through the Holy Spirit. Joseph her husband, since he was a righteous man, yet unwilling to expose her to shame, decided to divorce her quietly. Such was his intention when, behold, the angel of the Lord appeared to him in a dream and said, "Joseph, son of David, do not be afraid to take Mary your wife into your home. For it is through the Holy Spirit that this child has been conceived in her. She will bear a son and you are to name him Jesus, because he will save his people from their sins." All this took place to fulfill what the Lord had said through the prophet: / *Behold, the virgin shall conceive and bear a son, / and they shall name him Emmanuel, /* which means "God is with us." When Joseph awoke, he did as the angel of the Lord had commanded him and took his wife into his home.

Brief Silence

For Reflection

This Sunday's gospel is an annunciation to Joseph that Mary would conceive and bear a Son by the Holy Spirit: the "birth of Jesus Christ came about . . . through the Holy Spirit." Yet, by God's choice, the collaboration of an ordinary man and an ordinary woman was necessary. Joseph and Mary heard God's word announcing salvation and obeyed it. Through such divine-human collaboration Jesus became "Emmanuel . . . God is with us." Here is the Good News of the gospel: by such a simple act as Joseph's obeying God's messenger and taking "his wife into his home," God is with us in the incarnated Son. If God chose such simple folk as Joseph and Mary to incarnate the divine Son, is it not reasonable to think that Son's continued presence in the world is brought about by us? Thus, the Incarnation is not limited to a single event we celebrate annually in December, but happens every day in the ordinary circumstances of our own lives.

In this Good News of God's choosing to use simple, human folk to cooperate with the divine plan for salvation, we experience the great dignity God affords us human beings who hear and obey him. We are raised up, not only because God became incarnate and shared in our humanity in every way except sin, but also because God chooses us to continue that divine presence in the world!

✦ Eucharist announces and makes present *Emmanuel*, "God is with us." My daily life is a living Eucharist for others whenever I . . .

Brief Silence

Prayer

God, who is ever present to us, strengthen us to follow your commands as did Joseph, and to be open to all you ask of us. We ask this through Christ our Lord. **Amen.**

THE NATIVITY OF THE LORD

Christmas celebrates a great mystery: here in our everyday lives and ministry our God comes to us. Let us open our hearts to this mystery of redemption . . .

Prayer

O wondrous God, your divine Son was born of the Virgin Mary, who wrapped him in swaddling clothes and laid him in a manger. Help us always to make room for his presence in our hearts and to share that presence with others. We ask this through Christ our Lord. **Amen.**

Gospel (Luke 2:1-14; from the Mass at Midnight)

In those days a decree went out from Caesar Augustus that the whole world should be enrolled. This was the first enrollment, when Quirinius was governor of Syria. So all went to be enrolled, each to his own town. And Joseph too went up from Galilee from the town of Nazareth to Judea, to the city of David that is called Bethlehem, because he was of the house and family of David, to be enrolled with Mary, his betrothed, who was with child. While they were there, the time came for her to have her child, and she gave birth to her firstborn son. She wrapped him in swaddling clothes and laid him in a manger, because there was no room for them in the inn.

Now there were shepherds in that region living in the fields and keeping the night watch over their flock. The angel of the Lord appeared to them and the glory of the Lord shone around them, and they were struck with great fear. The angel said to them, "Do not be afraid; for behold, I proclaim to you good news of great joy that will be for all the people. For today in the city of David a savior has been born for you who is Christ and Lord. And this will be a sign for you: you will find an infant wrapped in swaddling clothes and lying in a manger." And suddenly there was a multitude of the heavenly host with the angel, praising God and saying: / "Glory to God in the highest / and on earth peace to those on whom his favor rests."

Brief Silence

For Reflection

The announcing angel revealed to fearful and startled shepherds "good news of great joy": the birth in Bethlehem of a Child who is "Christ and Lord." The heavenly host responded by bursting into songs of praise, glorifying God in heaven and announcing God's peace and favor on earth. The Incarnation does not leave humanity untouched. Those who respond to the startling revelation that "a savior has been born" for us are enabled to share in divine glory. Truly, this birth is like no other. The Incarnation is more than what happens to the divine Son; his taking on human flesh brings all God's creatures to sing a chorus of endless "Glory to God in the highest." The Good News and glad tidings includes our own response to God's wondrous deeds of salvation.

Christmas tends to bring out the best in us: we hear God's revelation of salvation and we respond with glory and praise. However, the real challenge of this gospel is to carry it forth beyond Christmas into our whole year. Each time we respond to God and conform our own will to the divine will, Christmas happens. Each time we reach out to those in need, Christmas happens. Each time we take time to be present to another, Christmas happens. In all these and in countless other simple acts of putting others ahead of ourselves, we lift ourselves to join in the song of the heavenly host, that unceasing chorus of praise and glory. Glory to God in the highest!

✦ Surprisingly, the "Christ and Lord" is found "lying in the manger." Some of the surprising places or times I have experienced Christ's incarnation are . . .

Brief Silence

Prayer

O God of salvation, you give us great joy as we celebrate the birth of your divine Son. Receive our praise and thanksgiving, and help us to grow in our love for you. We ask this through Christ our Lord. **Amen.**

THE HOLY FAMILY OF JESUS, MARY, AND JOSEPH

The feast of the Holy Family reminds us that holiness for families is not dependent upon perfection or easy roads. As Mary and Joseph show us, holiness is dependent upon faithful obedience to God. Let us reflect on how faithful we have been to doing God's will . . .

Prayer

O God, you protect with care those whom you love. May we grow in holiness, may our families be strong and virtuous, and may we always obey your holy will. We ask this through Christ our Lord. **Amen.**

Gospel (Matt 2:13-15, 19-23)

When the magi had departed, behold, the angel of the Lord appeared to Joseph in a dream and said, "Rise, take the child and his mother, flee to Egypt, and stay there until I tell you. Herod is going to search for the child to destroy him." Joseph rose and took the child and his mother by night and departed for Egypt. He stayed there until the death of Herod, that what the Lord had said through the prophet might be fulfilled, *Out of Egypt I called my son.*

When Herod had died, behold, the angel of the Lord appeared in a dream to Joseph in Egypt and said, "Rise, take the child and his mother and go to the land of Israel, for those who sought the child's life are dead." He rose, took the child and his mother, and went to the land of Israel. But when he heard that Archelaus was ruling over Judea in place of his father Herod, he was afraid to go back there. And because he had been warned in a dream, he departed for the region of Galilee. He went and dwelt in a town called Nazareth, so that what had been spoken through the prophets might be fulfilled, *He shall be called a Nazorean.*

Brief Silence

DECEMBER 30, 2007

For Reflection

Holiness is not a misty-eyed, other-worldly mode of living. Rather, it is a realistic engagement in the difficulties, struggles, and tensions of human life and relating. Our modern families are like the Holy Family in that, as they did, we also face challenges in responding to God faithfully and obediently. The holiness of a family is not dependent upon perfection or an easy road. As Mary and Joseph showed us, holiness is dependent upon faithfulness and obedience to God's messages.

Whether we are a traditional family or a single parent family, whether we have biological or adopted or foster children or no children, whether we live in an expensive home or a subsidized rental unit makes no difference for living as a holy family. What does make a difference is hearing God's message and doing God's will. Hearing God's message and responding to God's will made the Holy Family holy; it makes our families holy too. This is gospel living: responding with fidelity and obedience both to hardships and to God's wonderful gifts of grace. Sometimes it is the very hardships that help us put our priorities straight and realize how dependent upon our loving God we really are.

✦ For those who are experiencing distress or peril, I am like eucharistic sustenance for them whenever I . . .

Brief Silence

Prayer

Gracious God, you nourish us for our own journey through life. Be with us always as we struggle to hear and follow your will. We ask this through Christ our Lord. **Amen.**

SOLEMNITY OF THE BLESSED VIRGIN MARY, MOTHER OF GOD

It is fitting that we honor Mary, the Mother of God; may we draw closer to the Son she bore and be his presence for others . . .

Prayer
O ever-living God, you blessed Mary with a heart of receptivity and reflection. May we be as loving as Mary, ponder the great mystery of your saving love, and keep your Son close to us as Mary cared for her Son. We ask this through Christ our Lord. **Amen**.

Gospel (Luke 2:16-21)
The shepherds went in haste to Bethlehem and found Mary and Joseph, and the infant lying in the manger. When they saw this, they made known the message that had been told them about this child. All who heard it were amazed by what had been told them by the shepherds. And Mary kept all these things, reflecting on them in her heart. Then the shepherds returned, glorifying and praising God for all they had heard and seen, just as it had been told to them.

When eight days were completed for his circumcision, he was named Jesus, the name given him by the angel before he was conceived in the womb.

Brief Silence

For Reflection

This New Year offers us yet another opportunity to resolve to recognize God's many overtures of presence to us. Like Mary, our contemplative stance toward God's revelations brings us to see God in the grateful, smiling gurgle of the baby who has just been changed and comforted; to see God in the need of the street person asking for alms; to see God in the lonely elderly begging for a chat. Thus do our active participation in salvation and our contemplative response come together. We see God's presence in the quiet, little responses to others.

When we wish each other "Happy New Year" as Christians, as members of the Body of Christ participating in Christ's dying and rising mystery, we are really wishing each other a grace-filled year of responding to God's revelation and a year of contemplating what we have seen and heard so that we can come to understand with more depth and insight. The challenge of this day, then, is that our "Happy New Year" be more than a passing greeting. It must also be a pledge to, like the shepherds and Mary, embrace in joy and peace God's presence to us and in us.

✦ "Mary kept all these things, reflecting on them in her heart." Practices that help me develop a more contemplative posture to my faith and daily living are . . .

Brief Silence

Prayer

O God, you are worthy of all glory and praise. As we honor Mary, the mother of your divine Son, help us to be like her and contemplate in our hearts your marvelous deeds on our behalf. We ask this through Christ our Lord. **Amen.**

THE EPIPHANY OF THE LORD

The feast of the Epiphany celebrates Jesus, the Light of the world, being manifested to the Magi from the East. Let us offer God our homage through Christ who is our Light . . .

Prayer

O God, you guide us by the light of your wisdom to encounter your Son in the ordinary circumstances of our daily lives. Help us to follow him faithfully to everlasting glory. We ask this through Christ our Lord. **Amen**.

Gospel (Matt 2:1-12)

When Jesus was born in Bethlehem of Judea, in the days of King Herod, behold, magi from the east arrived in Jerusalem, saying, "Where is the newborn king of the Jews? We saw his star at its rising and have come to do him homage." When King Herod heard this, he was greatly troubled, and all Jerusalem with him. Assembling all the chief priests and the scribes of the people, he inquired of them where the Christ was to be born. They said to him, "In Bethlehem of Judea, for thus it has been written through the prophet: / *And you, Bethlehem, land of Judah, / are by no means least among the rulers of Judah; / since from you shall come a ruler, / who is to shepherd my people Israel.*" / Then Herod called the magi secretly and ascertained from them the time of the star's appearance. He sent them to Bethlehem and said, "Go and search diligently for the child. When you have found him, bring me word, that I too may go and do him homage." After their audience with the king they set out. And behold, the star that they had seen at its rising preceded them, until it came and stopped over the place where the child was. They were overjoyed at seeing the star, and on entering the house they saw the child with Mary his mother. They prostrated themselves and did him homage. Then they opened their treasures and offered him gifts of gold, frankincense, and myrrh. And having been warned in a dream not to return to Herod, they departed for their country by another way.

Brief Silence

JANUARY 6, 2008

For Reflection

The pattern of our own lives is that of the Magi: receive God's revelation, seek the Light, encounter the Savior, offer homage. An important lesson here for living is that authentic homage (that is, worship) naturally flows from following the Light of Christ in our daily living. Worship, then, is more than what happens in church on Sunday. It flows from the light of our own selves that shines throughout our weekdays, witnessing to our own encounters with the Light. Our very living must proclaim the goodness of the Lord by the good we do for others.

Receiving God's revelation and responding faithfully always demands of us self-giving. Just as the Magi set out on a journey following the star, so is our own Christian journey about following the Light of Christ in all we do, even when it brings us to the Cross. The real challenge of this feast is not simply about following the light of a star to "the newborn king of the Jews" (gospel). It is about where one's heart lies. As the light of Christ shines on us, we are invited to see what lies deep within our own hearts, to bring forth what is good, and to offer ourselves in worship.

◆ The Eucharist memorializes Christ's great act of opening his treasure (his very life) to the Father. What helps me to open myself in homage to God as a living treasure is . . .

Brief Silence

Prayer

Bounteous God, you give us all good gifts so that we might come into your presence. Help us to open our hearts to others and in that act of self-giving give you thanks and praise. We ask this through Christ our Lord. **Amen.**

THE BAPTISM OF THE LORD

We celebrate on this feast of Jesus' baptism his identity as the beloved Son being made known and his mission to save the world being inaugurated. Let us recall our own baptismal identity and mission, and ask God to keep us faithful to being beloved sons and daughters of God . . .

Prayer
O God, your love for your divine Son was revealed at his baptism. Touch us always with your love, and help us to love others with openness and generosity. We ask this through Christ our Lord. **Amen.**

Gospel (Matt 3:13-17)
Jesus came from Galilee to John at the Jordan to be baptized by him. John tried to prevent him, saying, "I need to be baptized by you, and yet you are coming to me?" Jesus said to him in reply, "Allow it now, for thus it is fitting for us to fulfill all righteousness." Then he allowed him. After Jesus was baptized, he came up from the water and behold, the heavens were opened for him, and he saw the Spirit of God descending like a dove and coming upon him. And a voice came from the heavens, saying, "This is my beloved Son, with whom I am well pleased."

Brief Silence

JANUARY 13, 2008

For Reflection

In our culture the economy identifies us as consumers, and our mission is to buy. The entertainment industry identifies us as spectators, and our mission is to "tune in." Baptism identifies us as God's beloved children, and our mission is to follow Jesus. The symbolism of the water already says how our own identity is to play itself out in our mission. Plunged into the baptismal waters, we die to our old self; rising from the waters, we enter into the new life baptism promises. Baptism inaugurates us into the paschal mystery of Jesus Christ.

This dying and rising is the "stuff" of our Christian living. What enables us to continue to say yes to such living is that we know the dying always leads to rising, death always brings life. We know this with certainty because Jesus was baptized, his identity as beloved Son was revealed, he was faithful to his mission to bring forgiveness and justice, he died and then rose. The pattern of Jesus' life is the pattern of our own lives. Gospel living is as concrete as Jesus' life and mission. Like Jesus, we do good when we forgive; we heal others when we offer kind words instead of words that tear down or help another without being asked.

◆ Eucharist is where I experience again and again that all the baptized are God's "beloved . . . with whom [God is] well pleased." One way I could share this with another this week is . . .

Brief Silence

Prayer

Loving God, your Spirit descended upon Jesus and strengthened him for his saving mission. May that same Spirit come upon us and strengthen us to continue Jesus' work of salvation. We ask this through Christ our Lord. **Amen.**

SECOND SUNDAY IN ORDINARY TIME

In this Sunday's gospel John the Baptist testifies to his understanding of who Jesus is. May we come to know this Jesus more intimately and give testimony in our lives to his love and presence . . .

Prayer

O God, you are present to us and desire to be known by us. Help us to encounter you in the ordinary circumstances of our lives and faithfully testify to all the deeds of salvation you have done for us. We ask this through Christ our Lord. **Amen.**

Gospel (John 1:29-34)

John the Baptist saw Jesus coming toward him and said, "Behold, the Lamb of God, who takes away the sin of the world. He is the one of whom I said, 'A man is coming after me who ranks ahead of me because he existed before me.' I did not know him, but the reason why I came baptizing with water was that he might be made known to Israel." John testified further, saying, "I saw the Spirit come down like a dove from heaven and remain upon him. I did not know him, but the one who sent me to baptize with water told me, 'On whomever you see the Spirit come down and remain, he is the one who will baptize with the Holy Spirit.' Now I have seen and testified that he is the Son of God."

Brief Silence

For Reflection

John the Baptist unveils in his relationship to Christ the posture of the church, which is to go from not knowing to seeing to testifying. We don't come to a one-time understanding of Christ. Our whole lives are spent beholding the Lamb of God, and in this very encounter we receive the Spirit and are commissioned to carry on Jesus' saving mission. The surprise of this gospel is that, as the Father entrusted to the beloved Son the work of salvation, Jesus entrusts *to us* this same saving mission by baptizing us with the Holy Spirit.

Our baptismal task is continually to deepen our own understanding of who Jesus is and to make him known, and to deepen our own understanding of our Christian identity as the beloved daughters and sons of God, as the Body of Christ. Like John, we go from not knowing to seeing to testifying. More than likely, we aren't called to testify to the Son of God by going out and baptizing or doing great things. We testify to Jesus' identity and carry forth his saving mission by being faithful to the ordinary things in life, by doing God's will. The revelation of Jesus' identity—how he is made known in the world—is mediated by the way we live the Gospel daily.

✦ My faith journey, like John's, is a movement from "I did not know him" to "I have seen and testified." The Eucharist sustains me on that journey by . . . Ways I minister to others on that journey are . . .

Brief Silence

Prayer

Gracious God, you adopt us as your sons and daughters to continue the saving work of Christ. Help us to be faithful in making Christ known through the good we do for others. We ask this through Christ our Lord. **Amen.**

THIRD SUNDAY IN ORDINARY TIME

At this very moment, in the midst of our daily struggles and joys, Jesus calls us to follow him. May we always hear God's call and be faithful in following Jesus as his disciples . . .

Prayer

Amazing and wonderful God, you call us to be disciples and to teach the Gospel by the goodness of our lives. Help us to be faithful to this great mission and to be grateful for all with which you have entrusted us. We ask this through Christ our Lord. **Amen**.

Gospel (Matt 4:12-23 or 4:12-17)

When Jesus heard that John had been arrested, he withdrew to Galilee. He left Nazareth and went to live in Capernaum by the sea, in the region of Zebulun and Naphtali, that what had been said through Isaiah the prophet might be fulfilled: / *Land of Zebulun and land of Naphtali, / the way to the sea, beyond the Jordan, / Galilee of the Gentiles, / the people who sit in darkness have seen a great light, / on those dwelling in a land overshadowed by death / light has arisen.* From that time on, Jesus began to preach and say, "Repent, for the kingdom of heaven is at hand."

As he was walking by the Sea of Galilee, he saw two brothers, Simon who is called Peter, and his brother Andrew, casting a net into the sea; they were fishermen. He said to them, "Come after me, and I will make you fishers of men." At once they left their nets and followed him. He walked along from there and saw two other brothers, James, the son of Zebedee, and his brother John. They were in a boat, with their father Zebedee, mending their nets. He called them, and immediately they left their boat and their father and followed him. He went around all of Galilee, teaching in their synagogues, proclaiming the gospel of the kingdom, and curing every disease and illness among the people.

Brief Silence

For Reflection

The preaching of Jesus and the call to discipleship that he issues take place in a particular time and setting. Neither is incidental: John has been arrested and the "land [is] overshadowed by death." It is at this time that Jesus announces that "the kingdom of heaven is at hand" and in this place that he calls his first disciples. Darkness and death do not thwart Jesus' ministry; rather, they are the reason for it. This gospel context foretells Jesus' destiny as well as our own.

As Jesus begins his public ministry, he issues two simple commands: "repent" and "come after me." As simple as these sound, they embody the radical demands of discipleship. Both demands are made urgent for the same reason: "the kingdom of God is at hand." The religious expectation of the time was that God's saving work would originate from the holy city of Jerusalem and be accomplished by a great and powerful messiah. Instead, we find an itinerant preacher in Gentile territory inaugurating God's kingdom. The kingdom of God is not a place, but is the recognition of God's just and rightful rule over all creation. This is the same saving ministry to which Jesus' disciples were called; it is our own ministry.

✦ This week as I reach out to someone who is distressed or in need of comfort, what helps me to remember that my encounter is a living Eucharist manifesting "the kingdom of heaven is at hand" is . . .

Brief Silence

Prayer

Merciful God, your kingdom is manifested in the good we do for others. Help us to repent of all that keeps us from growing closer to you and to respond faithfully to your call to live the Gospel. We ask this through Christ our Lord. **Amen.**

FOURTH SUNDAY IN ORDINARY TIME

In this Sunday's gospel Jesus looks over the crowds and sees them as blessed. May we come to realize more deeply our own blessedness in Christ . . .

Prayer

O God, you are the One in whom we rejoice and are glad. Bless us with your divine care and help us to be faithful to the call of the Beatitudes. We ask this through Christ our Lord. **Amen.**

Gospel (Matt 5:1-12a)

When Jesus saw the crowds, he went up the mountain, and after he had sat down, his disciples came to him. He began to teach them, saying: / "Blessed are the poor in spirit, / for theirs is the kingdom of heaven. / Blessed are they who mourn, / for they will be comforted. / Blessed are the meek, / for they will inherit the land. / Blessed are they who hunger and thirst for righteousness, / for they will be satisfied. / Blessed are the merciful, / for they will be shown mercy. / Blessed are the clean of heart, / for they will see God. / Blessed are the peacemakers, / for they will be called children of God. / Blessed are they who are persecuted for the sake of righteousness, / for theirs is the kingdom of heaven. / Blessed are you when they insult you and persecute you / and utter every kind of evil against you falsely because of me. / Rejoice and be glad, for your reward will be great in heaven."

Brief Silence

FEBRUARY 3, 2008

For Reflection

The gospel calls us to an encounter with Jesus. Note the opening verse: Jesus "went up the mountain," which perhaps for Matthew is a sign of Jesus' drawing nearer to God, since in the Old Testament theophanies often took place on mountains. In this context of the presence of the holy does Jesus begin to teach his disciples about their own holiness—blessedness. In our society, when asked about ourselves, we tend to respond with what we do—I'm an accountant, a teacher, an assembly line worker, a missionary. Yet, what is most important about us is *who we are*—blessed by God. Jesus "saw" the crowds in a way that others did not. Jesus looked at the people and saw the poor in spirit, the mournful, the meek, etc. as blessed. It is blessing that makes all these different people the same; all are blessed by God. This is our deepest identity—a people God has freely, generously, and readily blessed. Our following Jesus is a response to blessing.

Any action we might do (doing good for the sake of others is the cumulative effect of divine encounter) is motivated by being blessed. To this alternate vision of blessedness we must turn. We rejoice and are glad first in who we are—blessed. This is why the kingdom of heaven can be ours.

✦ Eucharist is the foretaste of the promised heavenly reward. I can share this hopeful, good news with those to whom I distribute Holy Communion and those whom I meet every day by . . .

Brief Silence

Prayer

Blessed are you, Lord God, for you give us all good things. Help us to live gracious and blessed lives, so that one day we might enjoy everlasting life with you. We ask this through Christ our Lord. **Amen.**

ASH WEDNESDAY

Lent begins, and so do our concerted efforts toward conversion. We are mindful that God is ever with us, strengthening our resolve to deepen our relationship with God, self, and others . . .

Prayer

Merciful God, you call us to prayer, fasting, and charity so that we might set right our relationships with you and others. Be with us as we journey through Lent toward new life, and help us to be faithful to our chosen practices of penance. We ask this through Christ our Lord. **Amen.**

Gospel (Matt 6:1-6, 16-18)

Jesus said to his disciples: "Take care not to perform righteous deeds in order that people may see them; otherwise, you will have no recompense from your heavenly Father. When you give alms, do not blow a trumpet before you, as the hypocrites do in the synagogues and in the streets to win the praise of others. Amen, I say to you, they have received their reward. But when you give alms, do not let your left hand know what your right is doing, so that your almsgiving may be secret. And your Father who sees in secret will repay you.

"When you pray, do not be like the hypocrites, who love to stand and pray in the synagogues and on street corners so that others may see them. Amen, I say to you, they have received their reward. But when you pray, go to your inner room, close the door, and pray to your Father in secret. And your Father who sees in secret will repay you.

"When you fast, do not look gloomy like the hypocrites. They neglect their appearance, so that they may appear to others to be fasting. Amen, I say to you, they have received their reward. But when you fast, anoint your head and wash your face, so that you may not appear to be fasting, except to your Father who is hidden. And your Father who sees what is hidden will repay you."

Brief Silence

For Reflection

This gospel calls us to work toward a consistency between our inner and outer selves, so that our actions truly express who we are before God. One of the challenges of Lent is that our Lenten practices authentically convey our seeking to be reconciled with God and each other, that our Lenten practices are not simply exercises we endure for forty days but are meaningful acts leading to genuine conversion of heart. There are three traditional facets of Christian penance: charity (or almsgiving), prayer, and fasting. The most authentic Christian penance incorporates all three because each of the three practices is directed in a different way to setting right our relationships with God, self, and others. Each of these three practices takes us outside and beyond ourselves: toward others through charity, toward God through prayer, toward ourselves through fasting.

Our Lenten penance need not be large and showy; in fact, it's better to undertake practices that are reasonably within our capacity at the same time that they stretch us beyond ourselves. A practical example might help: one could decide to say "thank you" at least once a day to another, and when doing so, remember that person is a member of the Body of Christ. One could agree to turn off the TV for five extra minutes and spend that time alone in prayer with God. One could decide to eat smaller portions, and in the feeling of being "less than full," recall that we are truly filled by God and God's gracious bestowal of graces.

✦ The three traditional practices of penance help me be a better extraordinary minister of Holy Communion in that . . .

Brief Silence

Prayer

O God, you strengthen sinners to repent and live the Good News. Help us to be honest with ourselves so that we can better serve others. We ask this through Christ our Lord. **Amen.**

FIRST SUNDAY OF LENT

As we begin Lent, the readings warn us about the dangers of temptation that lead to sin. Let us acknowledge that we have failed and beg God to help us live holier lives . . .

Prayer
Merciful God, your Son was like us in all things except sin. Help us to overcome our temptations to do wrong and to grow in our love for you. We ask this through Christ our Lord. **Amen**.

Gospel (Matt 4:1-11)
At that time Jesus was led by the Spirit into the desert to be tempted by the devil. He fasted for forty days and forty nights, and afterwards he was hungry. The tempter approached and said to him, "If you are the Son of God, command that these stones become loaves of bread." He said in reply, "It is written: / *One does not live on bread alone, / but on every word that comes forth / from the mouth of God.*"

Then the devil took him to the holy city, and made him stand on the parapet of the temple, and said to him, "If you are the Son of God, throw yourself down. For it is written: / *He will command his angels concerning you / and with their hands they will support you, / lest you dash your foot against a stone.*" / Jesus answered him, "Again it is written, *You shall not put the Lord, your God, to the test.*" Then the devil took him up to a very high mountain, and showed him all the kingdoms of the world in their magnificence, and he said to him, "All these I shall give to you, if you will prostrate yourself and worship me." At this, Jesus said to him, "Get away, Satan! It is written: / *The Lord, your God, shall you worship / and him alone shall you serve.*"

Then the devil left him and, behold, angels came and ministered to him.

Brief Silence

For Reflection

Jesus is led into the desert—a place of extreme desolation as well as a place of extreme beauty. Here, Jesus spends forty days and forty nights fasting and praying. Yes, Jesus walked every aspect of our human journey, even submitting himself to temptation and death. The three temptations the devil put to Jesus in the desert are not arbitrary—Jesus is faced with who he is and how he will carry on his saving mission.

We use the word "temptation" rather lightly in all kinds of contexts; for example, we say we are "tempted" to abandon our diet for a sumptuous dessert or "tempted" by a good sale to buy new clothes or "tempted" to go to a Saturday matinee rather than get some work finished around the house. But the nature of temptation described in this Sunday's gospel is much more serious, for its consequences involve our very life and salvation. Like the temptations the devil put to Jesus, we learn through our own struggle with good and evil that we live only by hearing God's word, trusting in God's presence, and worshiping God alone. In this way we come to salvation: by getting up close and seeing who we are and what God is asking of us.

✦ I am most tempted to . . . My ministry of distributing Holy Communion helps me face and overcome temptations in that . . .

Brief Silence

Prayer

God of truth and goodness, you have always nourished your people. Nourish us now so that we can overcome temptation and live in your presence always. We ask this through Christ our Lord. **Amen.**

SECOND SUNDAY OF LENT

Jesus took Peter, James, and John up to a mountaintop and was transfigured in glory before them. Let us repent of our sinfulness so that we too might share in Jesus' glory . . .

Prayer

Glorious God, you command that we listen to your Son. Help us to be faithful to the Gospel and to prepare for a share in transfigured glory by doing good for others. We ask this through Christ our Lord. **Amen.**

Gospel (Matt 17:1-9)

Jesus took Peter, James, and John his brother, and led them up a high mountain by themselves. And he was transfigured before them; his face shone like the sun and his clothes became white as light. And behold, Moses and Elijah appeared to them, conversing with him. Then Peter said to Jesus in reply, "Lord, it is good that we are here. If you wish, I will make three tents here, one for you, one for Moses, and one for Elijah." While he was still speaking, behold, a bright cloud cast a shadow over them, then from the cloud came a voice that said, "This is my beloved Son, with whom I am well pleased; listen to him." When the disciples heard this, they fell prostrate and were very much afraid. But Jesus came and touched them, saying, "Rise, and do not be afraid." And when the disciples raised their eyes, they saw no one else but Jesus alone.

As they were coming down from the mountain, Jesus charged them, "Do not tell the vision to anyone until the Son of Man has been raised from the dead."

Brief Silence

For Reflection

The vision and promise of glory is what sustains us in face of temptation and draws us forward on our journey of discipleship. The transfiguration is a foreshadowing of the fulfillment, the greater and permanent glory of Jesus' being "raised from the dead" after three days. Further, by our consistently choosing Christ, he becomes more manifest in our lives so we too share in this glory. Thus, the transfiguration of Christ foreshadows our own coming to glory.

We accept the gift when we "listen to him." But listening does more than promise glory; it reminds us that to reach that glory we must be willing to join Jesus in his passion and death as well. Our Christian journey is about listening to God's word, living a life of dying to self, and basking in the new life that comes to those who faithfully follow Jesus "up a high mountain" of transfiguration and promised glory—and also "down from the mountain" to the everyday temptations and self-giving. Why are we willing to walk this Christian journey? Because of the great hope we have in the outcome. We have been promised the same blessings of Abraham; and even more, we will be raised from the dead and have new life and immortality as Jesus died and rose from the dead to eternal glory.

✦ I received glimpses of promised glory when . . . This helps me be a better extraordinary minister of Holy Communion when . . .

Brief Silence

Prayer

Glorious God, your Son's face shone with the brilliance of the sun. Help us to be open to the light that is within us and to shine forth your goodness to us. We ask this through Christ our Lord. **Amen.**

THIRD SUNDAY OF LENT

In this Sunday's gospel Jesus encounters the Samaritan woman at the well and speaks with her at length. Let us acknowledge our sinfulness so that with pure hearts we might hear Jesus speaking to us . . .

Prayer

God of life, you sent your Son among us to be our Savior who brings us to belief. Give us living water so that we might deepen our faith and worship you with hearts filled with awe and wonder. We ask this through Christ our Lord. **Amen.**

Gospel (John 4:5-15, 19b-26, 39a, 40-42 [Longer Form: John 4:5-42])

Jesus came to a town of Samaria called Sychar, near the plot of land that Jacob had given to his son Joseph. Jacob's well was there. Jesus, tired from his journey, sat down there at the well. It was about noon.

 A woman of Samaria came to draw water. Jesus said to her, "Give me a drink." His disciples had gone into the town to buy food. The Samaritan woman said to him, "How can you, a Jew, ask me, a Samaritan woman, for a drink?"—For Jews use nothing in common with Samaritans.—Jesus answered and said to her, "If you knew the gift of God and who is saying to you, 'Give me a drink,' you would have asked him and he would have given you living water." The woman said to him, "Sir, you do not even have a bucket and the cistern is deep; where then can you get this living water? Are you greater than our father Jacob, who gave us this cistern and drank from it himself with his children and his flocks?" Jesus answered and said to her, "Everyone who drinks this water will be thirsty again; but whoever drinks the water I shall give will never thirst; the water I shall give will become in him a spring of water welling up to eternal life." The woman said to him, "Sir, give me this water, so that I may not be thirsty or have to keep coming here to draw water.

"I can see that you are a prophet. Our ancestors worshiped on this mountain; but you people say that the place to worship is in Jerusalem." Jesus said to her, "Believe me, woman, the hour is coming when you will worship the Father neither on this mountain nor in Jerusalem. You people worship what you do not understand; we worship what we understand, because salvation is from the Jews. But the hour is coming, and is now here, when true worshipers will worship the Father in Spirit and truth; and indeed the Father seeks such people to worship him. God is Spirit, and those who worship him must worship in Spirit and truth." The woman said to him, "I know that the Messiah is coming, the one called the Christ; when he comes, he will tell us everything." Jesus said to her, "I am he, the one who is speaking with you."

Many of the Samaritans of that town began to believe in him. When the Samaritans came to him, they invited him to stay with them; and he stayed there two days. Many more began to believe in him because of his word, and they said to the woman, "We no longer believe because of your word; for we have heard for ourselves, and we know that this is truly the savior of the world."

Brief Silence

THIRD SUNDAY OF LENT

For Reflection

This gospel story begins with a simple, human scene: a thirsty traveler, a communal well, a woman come to draw water. But something significant happens: the scene shifts from Jesus' thirst to that of the woman. The Samaritan woman thought she was thirsting for water; Jesus gradually reveals to her that she is thirsting for *living* water, a water only he can give because of who he truly is. Only during their extended conversation is Jesus' identity gradually revealed: as a Jewish man, then a prophet, then Messiah. Finally, the townspeople come to recognize Jesus as the "savior of the world."

The source of our own living waters is found in the baptismal font. There we are plunged into the death of Christ. There we receive a share in divine life. The living waters of baptism promise eternal life for those who are faithful to baptism's commitment and live faithfully their identity as members of the Body of Christ. We "thirst" when we distance ourselves from Christ and choose our own wills over God's. Our "thirst" is satisfied when we surrender ourselves to the refreshment of the living waters of God's word and live with Christ at the very center of our being. These living waters challenge us to acknowledge our sinfulness and find a new life in Christ. This is the conversion Lent opens for us. This is the conversation we must enter.

✦ The conversion I must undertake in order to be a better extraordinary minister of Holy Communion is . . . During this conversion journey, I thirst for . . .

Brief Silence

Prayer

Gracious God, you give us all we need in order to receive salvation. Help us to be open to all you offer us, to hear your word, and to live what we believe. We ask this through Christ our Lord. **Amen.**

FOURTH SUNDAY OF LENT

In the gospel Jesus comes to the man born blind and heals him. Lent is a time for us to beg for healing as we ask Jesus to open our eyes to our own need for repentance . . .

Prayer
Almighty God, no weakness is too great for you to heal. Bring us to healing waters, that we might come to deeper belief and more fervently worship you. We ask this through Christ our Lord. **Amen.**

Gospel (John 9:1, 6-9, 13-17, 34-38 [Longer Form: John 9:1-41])
As Jesus passed by he saw a man blind from birth. He spat on the ground and made clay with the saliva, and smeared the clay on his eyes, and said to him, "Go wash in the Pool of Siloam"—which means Sent—. So he went and washed, and came back able to see.

His neighbors and those who had seen him earlier as a beggar said, "Isn't this the one who used to sit and beg?" Some said, "It is," but others said, "No, he just looks like him." He said, "I am."

They brought the one who was once blind to the Pharisees. Now Jesus had made clay and opened his eyes on a sabbath. So then the Pharisees also asked him how he was able to see. He said to them, "He put clay on my eyes, and I washed, and now I can see." So some of the Pharisees said, "This man is not from God, because he does not keep the sabbath." But others said, "How can a sinful man do such signs?" And there was a division among them. So they said to the blind man again, "What do you have to say about him, since he opened your eyes?" He said, "He is a prophet."

They answered and said to him, "You were born totally in sin, and are you trying to teach us?" Then they threw him out.

When Jesus heard that they had thrown him out, he found him and said, "Do you believe in the Son of Man?" He answered and said, "Who is he, sir, that I may believe in him?" Jesus said to him, "You have seen him, and the one speaking with you is he." He said, "I do believe, Lord," and he worshiped him.

Brief Silence

For Reflection

Jesus is present in this Sunday's gospel only at the beginning and end of the story. In the larger, center portion of the story (where controversy is heightened), Jesus is not present at all; the focus is on the blind man who can now see. It is telling that the name of the pool where the man washed the mud off his eyes and regained his sight is "Siloam," which means "sent." It is the man born blind who is "sent" to bear the good news, come to believe, and witness to Jesus as One who comes from God.

In their first encounter, Jesus gives the blind man physical sight. But only in their second encounter are we told that Jesus gives the man much more: the eyes of faith by which he sees Jesus as the Son of Man. In both encounters it is Jesus who comes to the man, who is open to what Jesus has to offer. Jesus seeks out and asks, "Do you believe . . . ?" The restoration of the blind man's physical sight culminates in the spiritual insight (faith) that Jesus is the "Son of Man" worthy of worship. But getting to that point is difficult: he is unrecognized by friends, challenged by authorities, unsupported by parents, expelled from the synagogue. Yet with each obstacle his vision of faith is sharpened and his resolve is strengthened. Only spiritual insight attains the goal of faith: worship of Jesus.

✦ The obstacles that must be stripped from me so I can see with the eyes of faith are . . .

Brief Silence

Prayer

O God, you heal and forgive with patience and compassion. Open our eyes to the goodness around us, and heal us of whatever keeps us from growing in faith and love. We ask this through Christ our Lord. **Amen.**

FIFTH SUNDAY OF LENT

In this Sunday's gospel Jesus calls Lazarus forth from death to life. Let us acknowledge our sinfulness so that we too might come to new life . . .

Prayer

God of life, your divine Son had the power and compassion to bring Lazarus back to life. Help us to live for the sake of others, and may we ourselves gain everlasting life. We ask this through Christ our Lord. **Amen.**

Gospel (John 11:3-7, 17, 20-27, 33b-45 [Longer Form: John 11:1-45])

The sisters of Lazarus sent word to Jesus, saying, "Master, the one you love is ill." When Jesus heard this he said, "This illness is not to end in death, but is for the glory of God, that the Son of God may be glorified through it." Now Jesus loved Martha and her sister and Lazarus. So when he heard that he was ill, he remained for two days in the place where he was. Then after this he said to his disciples, "Let us go back to Judea."

When Jesus arrived, he found that Lazarus had already been in the tomb for four days. When Martha heard that Jesus was coming, she went to meet him; but Mary sat at home. Martha said to Jesus, "Lord, if you had been here, my brother would not have died. But even now I know that whatever you ask of God, God will give you." Jesus said to her, "Your brother will rise." Martha said, "I know he will rise, in the resurrection on the last day." Jesus told her, "I am the resurrection and the life; whoever believes in me, even if he dies, will live, and everyone who lives and believes in me will never die. Do you believe this?" She said to him, "Yes, Lord. I have come to believe that you are the Christ, the Son of God, the one who is coming into the world."

He became perturbed and deeply troubled, and said, "Where have you laid him?" They said to him, "Sir, come and see." And Jesus wept. So the Jews said, "See how he loved him." But some of them said, "Could not the one who opened the eyes of the blind man have done something so that this man would not have died?"

So Jesus, perturbed again, came to the tomb. It was a cave, and a stone lay across it. Jesus said, "Take away the stone." Martha, the dead man's sister, said to him, "Lord, by now there will be a stench; he has been dead for four days." Jesus said to her, "Did I not tell you that if you believe you will see the glory of God?" So they took away the stone. And Jesus raised his eyes and said, "Father, I thank you for hearing me. I know that you always hear me; but because of the crowd here I have said this, that they may believe that you sent me." And when he had said this, he cried out in a loud voice, "Lazarus, come out!" The dead man came out, tied hand and foot with burial bands, and his face was wrapped in a cloth. So Jesus said to them, "Untie him and let him go."

Now many of the Jews who had come to Mary and seen what he had done began to believe in him.

Brief Silence

FIFTH SUNDAY OF LENT

For Reflection

In the gospel account various people believe Jesus could have performed a miracle to heal Lazarus and spare him from death. They are deeply agitated when Jesus does not arrive until after Lazarus is dead and buried. What could Jesus do for the dead? Believing that Jesus could perform miracles did not prepare them for the astonishing revelation that he had power over death itself. Jesus' conversation with the disciples makes it clear that his actions are to lead us to a level quite beyond the literal. Jesus can surely heal; he has shown this over and over again in his ministry. From the depths of anguish he prays to his Father so the crowd "may believe that you sent me." Then Jesus calls out to Lazarus, he comes out, and Jesus commands those standing by to "untie him and let him go." All of these events bring "many of the Jews" to seeing and believing. The believing called forth from the crowd, however, is more than in a miracle worker. They come to believe that Jesus is "the Christ, the Son of God."

The story clearly has implications beyond Lazarus' return to life and bringing the crowd to belief. First of all, Lazarus' dying and being brought back to life foreshadows Jesus' and our journey from death to life. Even as amazing as the raising of Lazarus is, the full extent of Jesus' power over death would be revealed only in his resurrection and in ours.

✦ At Eucharist I receive "resurrection and life." I mediate this to others whenever I . . .

Brief Silence

Prayer

Gracious God, you raise us to new life in Jesus your Son. Bring us to conversion of life so that we might seek only what brings us to eternal life. We ask this through Christ our Lord. **Amen.**

PALM SUNDAY OF THE LORD'S PASSION

This Sunday we commemorate Jesus' triumphant entry into Jerusalem and hear the account of his suffering and death. As we prepare to enter this holiest of weeks, let us open ourselves to God's saving mystery . . .

Prayer

Almighty and ever-living God, your Son entered triumphantly into Jerusalem and was acclaimed as the Son of David. Help us always to acclaim him as our Lord and Savior. We ask this through Christ our Lord. **Amen.**

Gospel (Matt 27:11-54 [Longer Form: Matt 26:14–27:66])

Jesus stood before the governor, Pontius Pilate, who questioned him, "Are you the king of the Jews?" Jesus said, "You say so." And when he was accused by the chief priests and elders, he made no answer. Then Pilate said to him, "Do you not hear how many things they are testifying against you?" But he did not answer him one word, so that the governor was greatly amazed.

Now on the occasion of the feast the governor was accustomed to release to the crowd one prisoner whom they wished. And at that time they had a notorious prisoner called Barabbas. So when they had assembled, Pilate said to them, "Which one do you want me to release to you, Barabbas, or Jesus called Christ?" For he knew that it was out of envy that they had handed him over. While he was still seated on the bench, his wife sent him a message, "Have nothing to do with that righteous man. I suffered much in a dream today because of him." The chief priests and the elders persuaded the crowds to ask for Barabbas but to destroy Jesus. The governor said to them in reply, "Which of the two do you want me to release to you?" They answered, "Barabbas!" Pilate said to them, "Then what shall I do with Jesus called Christ?" They all said, "Let him be crucified!" But he said, "Why? What evil has he done?" They only shouted the louder, "Let him be crucified!" When Pilate saw that he was not succeeding at all, but that a riot was breaking out instead, he took water and washed his hands in the sight of the crowd, saying, "I am innocent of this man's blood. Look to it yourselves." And the whole people said in reply, "His blood be upon us and upon our children." Then he released Barabbas to them, but after he had Jesus scourged, he handed him over to be crucified.

Then the soldiers of the governor took Jesus inside the praetorium and gathered the whole cohort around him. They stripped off his clothes and threw a scarlet military cloak about him. Weaving a crown out of thorns, they placed it on his head, and a reed in his right hand. And kneeling before him, they mocked him, saying, "Hail, King of the Jews!" They spat upon him and took the reed and kept striking him on the head. And when they had mocked him, they stripped him of the cloak, dressed him in his own clothes, and led him off to crucify him.

As they were going out, they met a Cyrenian named Simon; this man they pressed into service to carry his cross.

And when they came to a place called Golgotha—which means Place of the Skull—, they gave Jesus wine to drink mixed with gall. But when he had tasted it, he refused to drink. After they had crucified him, they divided his garments by casting lots; then they sat down and kept watch over him there. And they placed over his head the written charge against him: This is Jesus, the King of the Jews. Two revolutionaries were crucified with him, one on his right and the other on his left. Those passing by reviled him, shaking their heads and saying, "You who would destroy the temple and rebuild it in three days, save yourself, if you are the Son of God, and come down from the cross!" Likewise the chief priests with the scribes and elders mocked him and said, "He saved others; he cannot save himself. So he is the king of Israel! Let him come down from the cross now, and we will believe in him. He trusted in God; let him deliver him now if he wants him. For he said, 'I am the Son of God.'" The revolutionaries who were crucified with him also kept abusing him in the same way.

PALM SUNDAY OF THE LORD'S PASSION

From noon onward, darkness came over the whole land until three in the afternoon. And about three o'clock Jesus cried out in a loud voice, *"Eli, Eli, lema sabachthani?"* which means, "My God, my God, why have you forsaken me?" Some of the bystanders who heard it said, "This one is calling for Elijah." Immediately one of them ran to get a sponge; he soaked it in wine, and putting it on a reed, gave it to him to drink. But the rest said, "Wait, let us see if Elijah comes to save him." But Jesus cried out again in a loud voice, and gave up his spirit.

Here all kneel and pause for a short time.

And behold, the veil of the sanctuary was torn in two from top to bottom. The earth quaked, rocks were split, tombs were opened, and the bodies of many saints who had fallen asleep were raised. And coming forth from their tombs after his resurrection, they entered the holy city and appeared to many. The centurion and the men with him who were keeping watch over Jesus feared greatly when they saw the earthquake and all that was happening, and they said, "Truly, this was the Son of God!"

Brief Silence

For Reflection

From the high of hosanna acclamation (gospel at the procession with palms) to the low of betrayal, denial, and abandonment, the two gospels on this Sunday capture the life and death of the paschal mystery, a mystery that explains the joy and suffering of our own lives. We are able to embrace this mystery because we know who showed us the obedience and submission that leads to risen life.

Few of us are faced with a choice of persecution and death in acclaiming Jesus as the Son of God. No less demanding, however, is the daily choice to live the Gospel's requirement that we die to ourselves for the sake of others. This is how we confess Jesus as the Son of God. This, rather than denial and abandonment, is how we come to stand at the cross with Christ. This is how we come to new life. Like the disciples, we also know who Jesus is. Every Sunday we make our profession of faith: "We believe in one Lord, Jesus Christ, the only Son of God . . ." This Palm Sunday we are invited to reflect on our own knowledge of who Jesus is and how well we confess to knowing him in our daily living. We must embrace the death of daily self-giving if we are to pass through death to new life.

✦ Many times those to whom I minister pray, "My God, my God, why have you forsaken me?" My ministry is like a *living* Eucharist and rouses others to deeper trust and hope whenever I . . .

Brief Silence

Prayer

God of mercy, you have power over life and death. Help us to choose life and to live the Gospel so that one day we might share everlasting life with you in heaven. We ask this through Christ our Lord. **Amen**.

HOLY THURSDAY EVENING MASS OF THE LORD'S SUPPER

On this holy night we remember in a special way Jesus' command that we should do as he did: Jesus modeled for us how to be loving servants. Let us reflect on how well we have loved and served others . . .

Prayer

Nourishing God, we remember and celebrate the gift of the Eucharist you have given us. Help us to be ever mindful of its fruits and demands. We ask this through Christ our Lord. **Amen.**

Gospel (John 13:1-15)

Before the feast of Passover, Jesus knew that his hour had come to pass from this world to the Father. He loved his own in the world and he loved them to the end. The devil had already induced Judas, son of Simon the Iscariot, to hand him over. So, during supper, fully aware that the Father had put everything into his power and that he had come from God and was returning to God, he rose from supper and took off his outer garments. He took a towel and tied it around his waist. Then he poured water into a basin and began to wash the disciples' feet and dry them with the towel around his waist. He came to Simon Peter, who said to him, "Master, are you going to wash my feet?" Jesus answered and said to him, "What I am doing, you do not understand now, but you will understand later." Peter said to him, "You will never wash my feet." Jesus answered him, "Unless I wash you, you will have no inheritance with me." Simon Peter said to him, "Master, then not only my feet, but my hands and head as well." Jesus said to him, "Whoever has bathed has no need except to have his feet washed, for he is clean all over; so you are clean, but not all." For he knew who would betray him; for this reason, he said, "Not all of you are clean."

So when he had washed their feet and put his garments back on and reclined at table again, he said to them, "Do you realize what I have done for you? You call me 'teacher' and 'master,' and rightly so, for indeed I am. If I, therefore, the master and teacher, have washed your feet, you ought to wash one another's feet. I have given you a model to follow, so that as I have done for you, you should also do."

Brief Silence

For Reflection
When Jesus "poured water into a basin and began to wash the disciples' feet," Peter clearly became comfortable with this gesture. He addressed Jesus as "Master," and "rightly so." What Peter was not prepared for was how Jesus would demonstrate being "Master" is to be. Peter could not imagine Jesus' washing his feet because he could not imagine the "Master" as a servant—not to be in a position of power over, but to be truly a master who is fully a servant. Jesus is the loving servant because he put aside status and expectations to relate to others in a way that lifts them up. In his very servanthood Jesus attests to the dignity of others. His gift of his Body and Blood is a supreme example of love and spending oneself for the good of others.

The import of this symbolic foot washing is that we, Jesus' followers, "should also do." This is a symbolic act—in our society today we are hardly expected to take a basin and begin washing the feet of our dinner guests. What is expected of faithful followers of Jesus is to recognize the dignity of all others, to be agents of fidelity and justice, to be inclusive in our relationships, to lift the burdens of others, to love without reserve and without expectations of reward or return.

✦ The grace and privilege of serving another are . . . I recognize this in my ministry when . . .

Brief Silence

Prayer
God our Father, your Son taught us to be servants of all. Help us to recognize and respond to the needs of others, to ease the pain all around us, and to bring a touch of warmth and compassion to all those we meet. We ask this through Christ our Lord. **Amen.**

EASTER SUNDAY

We have completed our Lenten observance and now we come to "celebrate the feast." We sing out our alleluias in praise of the God of our salvation. Let us turn our hearts to our risen Lord in praise and thanksgiving . . .

Prayer
Ever-living God, you raised your Son from death to risen life. Give us a share in that same life, and help us to ring out our alleluias in the joy of our daily living. We ask this through Christ our Lord. **Amen.**

Gospel (John 20:1-9)
On the first day of the week, Mary of Magdala came to the tomb early in the morning, while it was still dark, and saw the stone removed from the tomb. So she ran and went to Simon Peter and to the other disciple whom Jesus loved, and told them, "They have taken the Lord from the tomb, and we don't know where they put him." So Peter and the other disciple went out and came to the tomb. They both ran, but the other disciple ran faster than Peter and arrived at the tomb first; he bent down and saw the burial cloths there, but did not go in. When Simon Peter arrived after him, he went into the tomb and saw the burial cloths there, and the cloth that had covered his head, not with the burial cloths but rolled up in a separate place. Then the other disciple also went in, the one who had arrived at the tomb first, and he saw and believed. For they did not yet understand the Scripture that he had to rise from the dead.

Brief Silence

For Reflection

Perhaps more than any other Easter gospel, this one can speak to us. Unlike the synoptic parallels and the next account in John where there is an angelic presence announcing Jesus' resurrection and Jesus himself appears to Mary and the disciples (cf. Matt 28:1-10; Mark 16:1-8; Luke 24:1-12; John 20:11-22), this account leaves us with only hints of the resurrection. We also have the Scriptures, which tell us that "he had to rise from the dead." Like the disciples, we have no immediate evidence of Jesus' resurrection. Rather, that wondrous event is mediated to us in the same way as for those disciples long ago. For us, Jesus' risen presence is mediated through servant-disciples who by their witness to gospel living announce that Jesus is alive and with us.

Seeing and believing, we still do not understand. This seeming contradiction characterizes the Christian journey. Through the Scriptures and by the witness of faithful disciples, we gradually come to believe in the Good News that Jesus brought. We gradually learn to encounter Jesus in the ordinary circumstances of every day, seeing his risen presence in the goodness of others, in our worship and prayer, even in our very needs. These personal encounters strengthen our faith in the risen Lord, that he has not died in vain, and that we even now share in the new life his resurrection promises.

✦ I am like Mary Magdala at Jesus' resurrection when . . . I am like the beloved disciple at Jesus' resurrection when . . .

Brief Silence

Prayer
God of life and joy, you make us glad with this festival celebrating the risen life of your Son Jesus. Bring our joy to completion and help us live as faithful followers of Jesus. We ask this through Christ our Lord. **Amen.**

SECOND SUNDAY OF EASTER (DIVINE MERCY SUNDAY)

Through our baptism we receive Jesus' mission to continue to bring salvation to others. Let us ask God to help us be faithful to our baptismal commitment . . .

Prayer
O living God, you call us to belief and joy. May we always recognize your presence and adore your greatness. We ask this through Christ our Lord. **Amen.**

Gospel (John 20:19-31)
On the evening of that first day of the week, when the doors were locked, where the disciples were, for fear of the Jews, Jesus came and stood in their midst and said to them, "Peace be with you." When he had said this, he showed them his hands and his side. The disciples rejoiced when they saw the Lord. Jesus said to them again, "Peace be with you. As the Father has sent me, so I send you." And when he had said this, he breathed on them and said to them, "Receive the Holy Spirit. Whose sins you forgive are forgiven them, and whose sins you retain are retained."

Thomas, called Didymus, one of the Twelve, was not with them when Jesus came. So the other disciples said to him, "We have seen the Lord." But he said to them, "Unless I see the mark of the nails in his hands and put my finger into the nailmarks and put my hand into his side, I will not believe."

Now a week later his disciples were again inside and Thomas was with them. Jesus came, although the doors were locked, and stood in their midst and said, "Peace be with you." Then he said to Thomas, "Put your finger here and see my hands, and bring your hand and put it into my side, and do not be unbelieving, but believe." Thomas answered and said to him, "My Lord and my God!" Jesus said to him, "Have you come to believe because you have seen me? Blessed are those who have not seen and have believed."

Now, Jesus did many other signs in the presence of his disciples that are not written in this book. But these are written that you may come to believe that Jesus is the Christ, the Son of God, and that through this belief you may have life in his name.

Brief Silence

For Reflection

What does it mean to *believe* in the resurrection of Jesus? Like Thomas, many of us struggle with belief. Too often, however, our struggle is similar to Thomas': we want tangible evidence. The twist of the gospel lies in the kind of tangible evidence we are given: the tangible presence of the risen Jesus is found in *our being sent* to continue the mission of Jesus; the tangible evidence of the presence of the risen Jesus is found in receiving the Holy Spirit so we can do the good works of faithful disciples.

Coming to believe, then, means to stake our lives on the risen Jesus whom we have not seen and to accept a mission to the world. Jesus' resurrection has implications for more than just him: "As the Father has sent me, so *I send you.*" Jesus makes clear that for which we are sent: to see, believe, receive the Holy Spirit, forgive sins, have life. This is the gift of risen life Jesus gives us and that we bring to others. Risen life is the sheer joy of seeing Jesus present in ourselves who serve and in others whom we serve. Risen life is the sheer glory of sharing in the fruits of resurrection: the forgiveness and peace that strengthen the relationship we have with the risen One and with each other.

✦ My struggle with belief lies in . . . Others who have helped strengthen my belief are . . .

Brief Silence

Prayer

God of the resurrection, you entrust us with the saving mission of your Son. Help us to be faithful disciples, and by the goodness of our lives bring others to belief. We ask this through Christ our Lord. **Amen.**

THIRD SUNDAY OF EASTER

Through Scripture and the breaking of the bread Jesus shared his new life with the disciples. We hope to have that new life renewed within us as we ask God to bless us . . .

Prayer

Gracious God, through word and sacrament you bring us to everlasting life. Help us to recognize Jesus not only in the Eucharist we share but also in the ministry we do. We ask this through Christ our Lord. **Amen**.

Gospel (Luke 24:13-35)

That very day, the first day of the week, two of Jesus' disciples were going to a village seven miles from Jerusalem called Emmaus, and they were conversing about all the things that had occurred. And it happened that while they were conversing and debating, Jesus himself drew near and walked with them, but their eyes were prevented from recognizing him. He asked them, "What are you discussing as you walk along?" They stopped, looking downcast. One of them, named Cleopas, said to him in reply, "Are you the only visitor to Jerusalem who does not know of the things that have taken place there in these days?" And he replied to them, "What sort of things?" They said to him, "The things that happened to Jesus the Nazarene, who was a prophet mighty in deed and word before God and all the people, how our chief priests and rulers both handed him over to a sentence of death and crucified him. But we were hoping that he would be the one to redeem Israel; and besides all this, it is now the third day since this took place. Some women from our group, however, have astounded us: they were at the tomb early in the morning and did not find his body; they came back and reported that they had indeed seen a vision of angels who announced that he was alive. Then some of those with us went to the tomb and found things just as the women had described, but him they did not see." And he said to them, "Oh, how foolish you are! How slow of heart to believe all that the prophets spoke! Was it not necessary that the Christ should suffer these things and enter into his glory?" Then beginning with Moses and all the prophets, he interpreted to them what referred to him in all the Scriptures. As they approached the village to which they were going, he gave the impression that he was going on farther. But they urged him, "Stay with us, for it is nearly evening and the day is almost over." So he went in to stay with them. And it happened that, while he was with them at table, he took bread, said the blessing, broke it, and gave it to them. With that their eyes were opened and they recognized him, but he vanished from their sight. Then they said to each other, "Were not our hearts burning within us while he spoke to us on the way and opened the Scriptures to us?" So they set out at once and returned to Jerusalem where they found gathered together the eleven and those with them who were saying, "The Lord has truly been raised and has appeared to Simon!" Then the two recounted what had taken place on the way and how he was made known to them in the breaking of the bread.

Brief Silence

THIRD SUNDAY OF EASTER

For Reflection

Ever the servant, Jesus ministers to the disciples on their way to Emmaus by opening for them the Scriptures and opening their eyes to recognize him in the breaking of the bread. Jesus facilitated through word and deed a genuine, personal *encounter*, and only by that encounter were Cleopas and his companion able to recognize Jesus as the risen One. Thus, the real issue on the road to Emmaus was not simply understanding the Scriptures or gaining more knowledge. The servant Jesus removed the barriers of their own expectations ("Was it not necessary that the Christ should suffer these things and enter into his glory?") so the disciples could recognize where to refocus their attention—on him, the risen One.

Like the disciples on the road to Emmaus, we must recognize Jesus, become servant disciples, and make the risen Christ known through our own words and deeds. But to do so, we must expand our vision; we must assess our expectations and refocus our lives on Jesus. We must invite him to "[s]tay with us." This kind of servant-hospitality is the prerequisite for servant-witness.

✦ Some examples of when Jesus opened me to his risen presence in the Scriptures or in the breaking of the bread are . . .

Brief Silence

Prayer

O God, you nourish us by the breaking of the bread so that we might witness to your Son's resurrection. Help us always to focus our lives on Jesus and be faithful in all he asks of us. We ask this through Christ our Lord. **Amen.**

FOURTH SUNDAY OF EASTER

Through the waters of baptism we enter into new life through Jesus the gate. Let us ask God to help us recognize Jesus and follow his call . . .

Prayer

Shepherd God, you know us as your own and call us by name. Protect us and guide us, that we may follow faithfully your Son to eternal life. We ask this through Christ our Lord. **Amen.**

Gospel (John 10:1-10)

Jesus said: "Amen, amen, I say to you, whoever does not enter a sheepfold through the gate but climbs over elsewhere is a thief and a robber. But whoever enters through the gate is the shepherd of the sheep. The gatekeeper opens it for him, and the sheep hear his voice, as the shepherd calls his own sheep by name and leads them out. When he has driven out all his own, he walks ahead of them, and the sheep follow him, because they recognize his voice. But they will not follow a stranger; they will run away from him, because they do not recognize the voice of strangers." Although Jesus used this figure of speech, the Pharisees did not realize what he was trying to tell them.

So Jesus said again, "Amen, amen, I say to you, I am the gate for the sheep. All who came before me are thieves and robbers, but the sheep did not listen to them. I am the gate. Whoever enters through me will be saved, and will come in and go out and find pasture. A thief comes only to steal and slaughter and destroy; I came so that they might have life and have it more abundantly."

Brief Silence

For Reflection

On this Fourth Sunday of Easter we celebrate what we have traditionally called "Good Shepherd Sunday." This year's gospel is particularly interesting in that the image for Jesus is, not primarily as shepherd, but as gate: "But whoever enters through the gate is the shepherd of the sheep." Twice in the gospel Jesus declares himself to be the gate. The twist of the gospel is that the gate is also a symbol for the shepherd—the gate itself is both a barrier and a protection. The image of the gate directs our attention to Jesus as the risen One who always recognizes us and cares for us (yes, Jesus is the Good Shepherd). Jesus declares himself to be the "gate." The gate is the dividing line between the threats of the outside world ("thieves and robbers") and the safety of the sheepfold. It is also the passageway from life lived in the shadow of death to the abundant life of the Good Shepherd. Everything hinges on the Gate.

During this Easter season we leisurely bask in the joy and promise of the resurrection. But this Sunday's gospel also reminds us that danger and death are always lurking near, even as we celebrate risen life. Initially, following Jesus will lead to insult, suffering, judgment, and the cross. But Easter always reminds us that it leads us even further—to abundant life (gospel).

✦ The significance to me and my ministry of Jesus describing himself as a gate is . . .

Brief Silence

Prayer

Gracious God, you shepherd and guide us in right paths. As we celebrate the risen life of your Son, help us to be faithful disciples witnessing to the joy of the resurrection.
We ask this through Christ our Lord.
Amen.

FIFTH SUNDAY OF EASTER

We renew our baptismal commitment every Easter to become one with Jesus and the Father, and with each other. Let us ask for the grace to continue growing in these relationships . . .

Prayer

God our Father, you have prepared for us a dwelling place of eternal life with you. Strengthen our belief, that we might follow faithfully Jesus who is our way and truth and life. We ask this through Christ our Lord. **Amen.**

Gospel (John 14:1-12)

Jesus said to his disciples: "Do not let your hearts be troubled. You have faith in God; have faith also in me. In my Father's house there are many dwelling places. If there were not, would I have told you that I am going to prepare a place for you? And if I go and prepare a place for you, I will come back again and take you to myself, so that where I am you also may be. Where I am going you know the way." Thomas said to him, "Master, we do not know where you are going; how can we know the way?" Jesus said to him, "I am the way and the truth and the life. No one comes to the Father except through me. If you know me, then you will also know my Father. From now on you do know him and have seen him." Philip said to him, "Master, show us the Father, and that will be enough for us." Jesus said to him, "Have I been with you for so long a time and you still do not know me, Philip? Whoever has seen me has seen the Father. How can you say, 'Show us the Father'? Do you not believe that I am in the Father and the Father is in me? The words that I speak to you I do not speak on my own. The Father who dwells in me is doing his works. Believe me that I am in the Father and the Father is in me, or else, believe because of the works themselves. Amen, amen, I say to you, whoever believes in me will do the works that I do, and will do greater ones than these, because I am going to the Father."

Brief Silence

APRIL 20, 2008

For Reflection

Jesus speaks of his "Father's house," "dwelling places," and "prepar[ing] a place." At first, we, like the disciples, might think of this as a physical location, a destination such as we could find if we knew "the way." Jesus, however, leads us to a deeper understanding when he reveals where he and the Father dwell: within one another. One surprise of the gospel is that Jesus' dwelling place is not a *space* but a *relationship*: "I am in the Father and the Father is in me." The way to this dwelling place is Jesus, who leads us into the heart of God. The gospel is challenging us to enter into a profound relationship with Jesus, which ultimately means we share a profound relationship with the Father as well.

Another surprise of the gospel is that there are, indeed, "many dwelling places"—as many as there are faithful disciples who are the spiritual house, the living stones, the presence of the risen Jesus for each other. The astounding message of the risen Jesus is that *we ourselves* are the *living*, risen Jesus! Jesus admonishes us to do the "works that I do." The first "work" is to open ourselves to God's indwelling—everything else depends on this.

✦ I come to the heart of God through my ministry when . . .
I experience myself already dwelling with God when . . .

Brief Silence

Prayer

Loving God, you call us to be your holy people and you prepare an eternal home for us. May our work always reflect your goodness and our lives your love. We ask this through Christ our Lord. **Amen.**

SIXTH SUNDAY OF EASTER

God pours divine love into our hearts through the Spirit and calls us to newness of life in Christ. Let us celebrate God's love and life as we renew our commitment to be faithful disciples . . .

Prayer

Loving God, you care for us and will not leave us orphans. Help us to remain in faithful relationship with you so that we may be strengthened by the Spirit to continue the saving work of the risen Jesus. We ask this through Christ our Lord. **Amen**.

Gospel (John 14:15-21)

Jesus said to his disciples: "If you love me, you will keep my commandments. And I will ask the Father, and he will give you another Advocate to be with you always, the Spirit of truth, whom the world cannot accept, because it neither sees nor knows him. But you know him, because he remains with you, and will be in you. I will not leave you orphans; I will come to you. In a little while the world will no longer see me, but you will see me, because I live and you will live. On that day you will realize that I am in my Father and you are in me and I in you. Whoever has my commandments and observes them is the one who loves me. And whoever loves me will be loved by my Father, and I will love him and reveal myself to him."

Brief Silence

For Reflection

This Sunday's gospel selection begins and ends with the invitation to love Jesus by keeping his commandments. But this gospel is not only about *our* love; even more so, it is about *God's* love for us. God does everything possible to share divine life with us, even to sending the Spirit. On our own it is impossible either to know God or love God. This is why the gospel is so reassuring when Jesus promises us the Spirit who "remains with [us], and will be in [us]." If we wish to grow in our love for God, we must first become attentive to the Spirit who dwells within us. We get to know the Spirit within us (who is really the presence of the risen Jesus in us) by taking sufficient time to be aware of the Beloved so near us.

One way to do this is by being faithful to prayer—not just saying prayers, but focusing on God's presence within. Prayer is an essential, daily practice that helps us become more attuned to God's loving presence. Another way to become aware of God's loving presence is by regularly remembering all God's goodness to us and cultivating grateful hearts. A third way is to see around us those who are being faithful to God's commandments and appreciate those acts as expressions of another's love for God. If we but see, Jesus reveals himself to us!

✦ The Eucharist demonstrates being loved by the Father and Jesus revealing himself to me by . . .

Brief Silence

Prayer

Loving God, your Spirit dwells within us and enables us to love you and one another. Increase our love so that one day we might remain forever in your loving embrace. We ask this through Christ our Lord. **Amen.**

THE ASCENSION OF THE LORD

We celebrate Jesus' ascending to the heavens to take his rightful position at the right hand of God. We also celebrate the ascension as paving the way for us to receive the Spirit. Let us open ourselves to this great mystery and reflect on how it shapes the way we live . . .

Prayer
Faithful God, your Son ascended into heaven and took his place at your right hand. Help us to worship you in all we do and be faithful to our mission to spread the Gospel. We ask this through Christ our Lord. **Amen.**

Gospel **(Matt 28:16-20)**
The eleven disciples went to Galilee, to the mountain to which Jesus had ordered them. When they saw him, they worshiped, but they doubted. Then Jesus approached and said to them, "All power in heaven and on earth has been given to me. Go, therefore, and make disciples of all nations, baptizing them in the name of the Father, and of the Son, and of the Holy Spirit, teaching them to observe all that I have commanded you. And behold, I am with you always, until the end of the age."

Brief Silence

For Reflection

Jesus' ascension into heaven is not a reward for what he did on earth but a return to his rightful place at the right hand of the Father. The ascension, like the resurrection, manifests the divinity and lordship of Christ. And here is another mystery we celebrate: when we acknowledge Christ as Lord, we are led to worship him and continue his work on earth ("make disciples of all nations"). But the twist of the gospel is this new presence of Jesus is, through the power of the Spirit, *within us* ("I am with you always, until the end of the age") and is manifested when we continue Jesus' saving work as his disciples.

We don't have to be mystics or theologians to do what the Spirit in us urges: witness, baptize, teach. We do this by letting the Spirit work through us in our daily lives. Jesus himself makes this work very concrete when he tells the disciples to teach all nations "to observe all that I have commanded you." Here the truism "actions speak louder than words" would be so applicable. Our best witnessing, baptizing, and teaching is through our own living. When we live God's commandments, others may be led to do the same. When we worship well, others may be led to do the same. When we are confident of God's message, others may be also.

✦ I am most aware of the Spirit *within me* when . . . The difference this makes in my life and ministry is . . .

Brief Silence

Prayer

O God, you raise up women and men in every age to witness to your mighty deeds of salvation. Grant us strength of conviction and truthfulness of living so that we might proclaim the Gospel well. We ask this through Christ our Lord. **Amen.**

SEVENTH SUNDAY OF EASTER

Our baptism plunges us into Christ's self-sacrificing mission. Let us prepare to do our ministry worthily so God may transform us into ever more perfect witnesses of his love and glory . . .

Prayer

O God, you are worthy of all glory and honor. Strengthen us to accomplish the work your Son has entrusted to us. We ask this through Christ our Lord. **Amen**.

Gospel (John 17:1-11a)

Jesus raised his eyes to heaven and said, "Father, the hour has come. Give glory to your son, so that your son may glorify you, just as you gave him authority over all people, so that your son may give eternal life to all you gave him. Now this is eternal life, that they should know you, the only true God, and the one whom you sent, Jesus Christ. I glorified you on earth by accomplishing the work that you gave me to do. Now glorify me, Father, with you, with the glory that I had with you before the world began.

"I revealed your name to those whom you gave me out of the world. They belonged to you, and you gave them to me, and they have kept your word. Now they know that everything you gave me is from you, because the words you gave to me I have given to them, and they accepted them and truly understood that I came from you, and they have believed that you sent me. I pray for them. I do not pray for the world but for the ones you have given me, because they are yours, and everything of mine is yours and everything of yours is mine, and I have been glorified in them. And now I will no longer be in the world, but they are in the world, while I am coming to you."

Brief Silence

For Reflection

This gospel is a portion of Jesus' priestly prayer for the disciples at the Last Supper, and the selection unfolds in two parts. The first part is a revelation of the intimate identity of Jesus with his Father, his fidelity to his mission, and Jesus' readiness to be glorified as he was "before the world began." The second part of the gospel is a reminder that Jesus glorified the Father "by accomplishing the work" that God gave him to do. For this, God glorified him in the resurrection. We also glorify Jesus by accomplishing the work Jesus has given us to do. In the course of doing this work, we know that we also share in his glory.

Indeed, God's life within us is already glorification. We normally think of our share in Jesus' glory as a future event that will happen after our natural death. But by the gift and presence of the Spirit in us, we already share in God's life. Yes, glorification is taking place even now! The Scripture message is so simple and clear: God is glorified when we take up Jesus' work. And in this we already share in Jesus' glory. Nevertheless, this assurance and promise of sharing in Jesus' glory ought not cloud our vision—a share in glory first entails a share in the self-giving sacrifice of Jesus as well.

✦ As I hear Jesus pray for his disciples (and for me!) in this gospel, I am moved to . . .

Brief Silence

Prayer

Glorious God, you call us to share your life and you entrust us with your Son's saving mission. Help us to accept all that Jesus has taught us and to be generously self-giving in our sharing this Good News with others. We ask this through Christ our Lord. **Amen.**

PENTECOST

We celebrate this Sunday the coming of the Spirit who empowers us to take up Christ's saving mission. Let us reflect on how the Spirit is present within us and helps us with our ministry . . .

Prayer

Empowering God, your Spirit comes upon us to strengthen us and guide us. Help us to be open to that same Spirit, respond to this grace, and be faithful in our serving others. We ask this through Christ our Lord. **Amen.**

Gospel (John 20:19-23)

On the evening of that first day of the week, for fear of the Jews, Jesus came and stood in their midst and said to them, "Peace be with you." When he had said this, he showed them his hands and his side. The disciples rejoiced when they saw the Lord. Jesus said to them again, "Peace be with you. As the Father has sent me, so I send you." And when he had said this, he breathed on them and said to them, "Receive the Holy Spirit. Whose sins you forgive are forgiven them, and whose sins you retain are retained."

Brief Silence

For Reflection

The re-creation of the Spirit is more than a share in Jesus' risen life and the bestowal of gifts. When Jesus appeared to the disciples "on that first day of the week . . . he showed them his hands and his side." By those wounds the disciples knew it was, indeed, their crucified Lord who is now glorified. Showing the disciples his wounds, however, is also a reminder that if we are to take up Jesus' mission through the power of the Spirit, we also will be wounded. Even Pentecost reminds us that the only way to share in Jesus' risen, glorified life is through death.

The risen Jesus appeared to the disciples and "showed them his hands and side." Jesus' showing his "hands and side" reveals to his disciples more than his identity as the crucified and risen One. In fact, it is because of his wounds we have peace, because of his wounds we have forgiveness, because of his wounds we have been given the Spirit. Wounds are the only way to peace and the only way faithfully to take up Jesus' saving mission. In our everyday self-giving for the good of others, we are showing our own hands and side—our own wounds for the sake of new life.

✦ My ministry "breathes" Christ's peace and Spirit upon those I encounter when . . .

Brief Silence

Prayer

God of power and might, you sent your Spirit to dwell within us. Enliven us with courage and self-giving, that we might minister faithfully and bring glory to your name. We ask this through Christ our Lord. **Amen.**

THE SOLEMNITY OF THE MOST HOLY TRINITY

The solemnity of the Most Holy Trinity is a day when we celebrate perhaps the most awesome of our Catholic mysteries. Let us pause in silence before our gracious God who chooses to love us and show us mercy, and who calls us into fellowship . . .

Prayer
O triune God, you are Father, Son, and Holy Spirit, three Persons in one God. Dwell within us, grant us salvation, and guide us to everlasting life with you. We ask this through Christ our Lord. **Amen.**

Gospel (John 3:16-18)
God so loved the world that he gave his only Son, so that everyone who believes in him might not perish but might have eternal life. For God did not send his Son into the world to condemn the world, but that the world might be saved through him. Whoever believes in him will not be condemned, but whoever does not believe has already been condemned, because he has not believed in the name of the only Son of God.

Brief Silence

MAY 18, 2008

For Reflection

Divine self-revelation was exceeded when God "gave his only Son" (gospel) so that we might be saved. But even more: the fullest revelation of the grace, love, and fellowship of the Trinity is extended to us believers with the sending of the Spirit as a share in divine intimacy—eternal life itself. The unceasing work of the Trinity is this: to love us into divine presence, into eternal life. Thus, the mystery and majesty of God is not kept internal to the community of divine Persons but is shared with us so that we might share in that very same divine life. At the same time that we are uplifted in praise, we are also brought down to earth by this solemnity for it reminds us that the only way we share in God's glory is to give of ourselves in the same way God gives to us: in love and mercy, graciousness and faithfulness.

Amazingly, our simple, good, everyday actions toward one another express the very life of God and God's desire for us. The mystery of the Trinity will always be mystery; nevertheless, we ourselves are privileged to express the wonder of divine life through our own goodness, mercy, love, and peace.

✦ My ministry of distributing Holy Communion is a reflection of the triune God in that . . .

Brief Silence

Prayer

God of goodness and peace, you reveal yourself to us through divine deeds of love. Help us to love one another and to deepen our relationships with you and each other. We ask this through Christ our Lord. **Amen.**

THE SOLEMNITY OF THE MOST HOLY BODY AND BLOOD OF CHRIST

We celebrate the gift that Jesus gives us in the Eucharist—his very Body and Blood. Let us pause and reflect on how we have been nourished by this gift and strengthened for self-giving . . .

Prayer

Nourishing God, you give us the Body and Blood of your divine Son to strengthen us on our journey to eternal life. Help us to grow in our appreciation for the gift of the Eucharist and to be that gift for others. We ask this through Christ our Lord. **Amen**.

Gospel (John 6:51-58)

Jesus said to the Jewish crowds: "I am the living bread that came down from heaven; whoever eats this bread will live forever; and the bread that I will give is my flesh for the life of the world."

The Jews quarreled among themselves, saying, "How can this man give us his flesh to eat?" Jesus said to them, "Amen, amen, I say to you, unless you eat the flesh of the Son of Man and drink his blood, you do not have life within you. Whoever eats my flesh and drinks my blood has eternal life, and I will raise him on the last day. For my flesh is true food, and my blood is true drink. Whoever eats my flesh and drinks my blood remains in me and I in him. Just as the living Father sent me and I have life because of the Father, so also the one who feeds on me will have life because of me. This is the bread that came down from heaven. Unlike your ancestors who ate and still died, whoever eats this bread will live forever."

Brief Silence

For Reflection

In the gospel Jesus describes himself as the "living bread" *given* for the "life of the world." This is what we memorialize in the Eucharist: that Jesus *gives* himself in his Body and Blood. Our participation in the Body and Blood of Christ demands that we, like Jesus, *give* ourselves for others. The core of the mystery of Eucharist—and of ourselves—is self-giving. It is a misunderstanding to conceive of Communion as a privatized moment between "Jesus and me" and that Communion is only about what each of us is given. Communion with the Body and Blood of Christ compels communion with one another.

It is no happenstance that self-giving is a necessary constituent of Eucharist—both in terms of Jesus' giving himself as Food for us and our giving ourselves to each other for the common good. It is also no happenstance that Eucharist is a share in the eschatological messianic banquet. Eucharist nourishes us and gives us the strength to choose self-giving sacrifice as a way of living, and this is the only way to achieve eternal life. No wonder we call ourselves a eucharistic people and no wonder Eucharist defines who we are as those baptized into Christ. By sharing in Jesus' Body and Blood we share in his cross and resurrection.

◆ My sharing in the eucharistic banquet and distributing the Eucharist motivates me to partake in the issues and problems within my community because . . .

Brief Silence

Prayer
Bounteous God, you feed us with the Bread of Life. Preserve us from all harm and strengthen us to do your will on our journey to everlasting life with you. We ask this through Christ our Lord. **Amen.**

NINTH SUNDAY IN ORDINARY TIME

In the gospel Jesus challenges his disciples to listen to his words and to act on them. Let us pray that we are attentive to God's word and faithful to our spirituality as ministers of Holy Communion . . .

Prayer

Lord God, your words guide us and bring us life. May we hear what you speak to us, be filled with your wisdom, and act faithfully in following your ways. We ask this through Christ our Lord. **Amen**.

Gospel (Matt 7:21-27)

Jesus said to his disciples: "Not everyone who says to me, 'Lord, Lord,' will enter the kingdom of heaven, but only the one who does the will of my Father in heaven. Many will say to me on that day, 'Lord, Lord, did we not prophesy in your name? Did we not drive out demons in your name? Did we not do mighty deeds in your name?' Then I will declare to them solemnly, 'I never knew you. Depart from me, you evildoers.'

"Everyone who listens to these words of mine and acts on them will be like a wise man who built his house on rock. The rain fell, the floods came, and the winds blew and buffeted the house. But it did not collapse; it had been set solidly on rock. And everyone who listens to these words of mine but does not act on them will be like a fool who built his house on sand. The rain fell, the floods came, and the winds blew and buffeted the house. And it collapsed and was completely ruined."

Brief Silence

For Reflection

In life we are faced with many choices, but the gospel informs us that there is one basic choice (the foundation, the rock) upon which all others must be made. That one choice is to live by Jesus' words and put into action what we have heard. Without this foundation, all other choices are like building our life on sand. In fact, the fundamental choice is for a life that does not collapse or a life that does collapse. The fundamental choice is for a life in obedience to God, a life with God at the center.

Unlike the examples of mighty deeds mentioned in the gospel (prophesying, driving out demons), what Jesus asks of us is simply to be faithful to his words and commandments in our everyday lives. Listening to his words may mean listening to another's cry for help; or it may mean that we spend some time alone in quiet prayer, being attentive to Jesus' abiding presence. Putting Jesus' words into practice may mean taking the time to be kind to a coworker; or it may mean sharing our abundance with those less fortunate. Building on rock ultimately means that we choose to give ourselves over for the good of another.

✦ My Christian life is like a rock for those to whom I minister when I . . .

Brief Silence

Prayer

God of our salvation, you are the rock upon which we build our lives. Be with us as we minister to others, so that we might bring them your word of strength and encouragement. We ask this through Christ our Lord. **Amen.**

TENTH SUNDAY IN ORDINARY TIME

Our loving and merciful God calls tax collectors and sinners to table fellowship. Let us reflect on the mercy and love God shows us by calling us to the table of the Eucharist and helping us serve that table well . . .

Prayer
God of mercy, you call all of us into your loving embrace. Help us not to judge the righteousness of others, but to welcome all as you welcome each of us. We ask this through Christ our Lord. **Amen.**

Gospel (Matt 9:9-13)
As Jesus passed on from there, he saw a man named Matthew sitting at the customs post. He said to him, "Follow me." And he got up and followed him. While he was at table in his house, many tax collectors and sinners came and sat with Jesus and his disciples. The Pharisees saw this and said to his disciples, "Why does your teacher eat with tax collectors and sinners?" He heard this and said, "Those who are well do not need a physician, but the sick do. Go and learn the meaning of the words, 'I desire mercy, not sacrifice.' I did not come to call the righteous but sinners."

Brief Silence

For Reflection

In the gospel for this Sunday Jesus calls the sinful, undesirable Matthew to follow him and then eats dinner in Matthew's house with "tax collectors and sinners." This action of Jesus raises table fellowship to a new level beyond hospitality and social occasion, as important as this is. Table fellowship becomes a symbol of the inclusivity of Jesus' call and the relationship in Jesus that we share together. Since Jesus excludes no one from the call, neither are we to exclude anyone from our homes and hearts.

The Pharisees "separated" (the Hebrew word "*phāras*" = to separate) themselves from others by their strict observance of the Law. Jesus demonstrates by his table fellowship "with tax collectors and sinners" that the deepest meaning of the Law is not separation but fellowship and mercy. The surprise of the gospel is that following Jesus as disciples is given a unique, concrete, everyday meaning: to share inclusive fellowship with sinners and outcasts. This means that discipleship is about establishing relationships with those whom it's easy to ignore and cast off. And we establish not just a minimum relationship, but one built on the intimacy and acceptance that we associate with table fellowship. The mercy Jesus desires and that we must practice is nothing less than the mercy God has shown us. We build our relationships and inclusivity on the pattern God has already established with us.

✦ Watching Jesus eat with tax collectors and sinners places on me the demand to . . .

Brief Silence

Prayer

Gracious God, you call us to your banquet table of love. Help us to love and care for others, that one day we might share everlasting joy with you. We ask this through Christ our Lord. **Amen.**

ELEVENTH SUNDAY IN ORDINARY TIME

This Sunday's gospel shows Jesus moved with pity when he sees the crowds troubled and abandoned. Let us open ourselves to God's compassion and mercy, so we can welcome and comfort the troubled and abandoned whom we meet . . .

Prayer

Compassionate God, you summon us to reach out to those in need and give us all we need to be compassionate as your Son Jesus has taught us. Be with us as we meet others, that we might ease their pain and bring forth joy and peace. We ask this through Christ our Lord. **Amen.**

Gospel **(Matt 9:36–10:8)**

At the sight of the crowds, Jesus' heart was moved with pity for them because they were troubled and abandoned, like sheep without a shepherd. Then he said to his disciples, "The harvest is abundant but the laborers are few; so ask the master of the harvest to send out laborers for his harvest."

Then he summoned his twelve disciples and gave them authority over unclean spirits to drive them out and to cure every disease and every illness. The names of the twelve apostles are these: first, Simon called Peter, and his brother Andrew; James, the son of Zebedee, and his brother John; Philip and Bartholomew, Thomas and Matthew the tax collector; James, the son of Alphaeus, and Thaddeus; Simon from Cana, and Judas Iscariot who betrayed him.

Jesus sent out these twelve after instructing them thus, "Do not go into pagan territory or enter a Samaritan town. Go rather to the lost sheep of the house of Israel. As you go, make this proclamation: 'The kingdom of heaven is at hand.' Cure the sick, raise the dead, cleanse lepers, drive out demons. Without cost you have received; without cost you are to give."

Brief Silence

For Reflection

In the gospel, Jesus looks upon the "troubled and abandoned" crowd and is "moved with pity." The Greek word for pity means "stirred to the bowels," moved to deep emotion, moved to compassion. This is one of the times in the gospels when we read of Jesus displaying great emotion. Without a leader, he knew the people would be lost. He came to find and save. The mission is urgent. Divine compassion is the wellspring of both call and mission. Jesus' deep compassion is manifested in his immediate response—he "summon[s] the twelve disciples" and sends them as ministers of his compassion, authorized to preach and heal in his name.

Jesus still calls and still sends. We ourselves are summoned to the abundant harvest as his laborers. We are authorized to continue his work which is, at root, a ministry of compassion. Like the Twelve, we have received divine compassion without cost (our call) and we are sent to give others that compassion we have received (our mission). This authority and power we have been given, however, is not for our own use, but so that the "kingdom of heaven" might be "at hand." The disciple is always called to do the work of the Master.

✦ I have been summoned to be an extraordinary minister of Holy Communion. In this ministry I do the work of the Master in that . . .

Brief Silence

Prayer

O God, you deeply desire to reach out to us in love and compassion. Touch us and heal us, so that we might reach out to others and meet their needs. We ask this through Christ our Lord. **Amen.**

TWELFTH SUNDAY IN ORDINARY TIME

In the gospel Jesus instructs us that he will acknowledge us before the Father when we confidently acknowledge Christ in our daily lives. Let us open ourselves to encounter Christ in the many ways he comes to us, so we can faithfully make him known . . .

Prayer

God of light, you bring joy to our hearts and dispel all fear. Receive from grateful hearts our love, and help us to be more caring toward others. We ask this through Christ our Lord. **Amen**.

Gospel (Matt 10:26-33)

Jesus said to the Twelve: "Fear no one. Nothing is concealed that will not be revealed, nor secret that will not be known. What I say to you in the darkness, speak in the light; what you hear whispered, proclaim on the housetops. And do not be afraid of those who kill the body but cannot kill the soul; rather, be afraid of the one who can destroy both soul and body in Gehenna. Are not two sparrows sold for a small coin? Yet not one of them falls to the ground without your Father's knowledge. Even all the hairs of your head are counted. So do not be afraid; you are worth more than many sparrows. Everyone who acknowledges me before others I will acknowledge before my heavenly Father. But whoever denies me before others, I will deny before my heavenly Father."

Brief Silence

JUNE 22, 2008

For Reflection

The gospel describes two opposing worlds: concealed/revealed, secret/known, darkness/light, whispered/proclaimed, kill body/cannot kill soul, small coin/worth more. Disciples can live in only one world and, if they are faithful, it is a world of danger. Why do we choose to be faithful and remain unafraid? Because God has announced our worth and will care for us. These images lend some concreteness to the demands of living the gospel (and liturgy). It is not enough to come to church Sunday after Sunday and hear the challenge of the gospel; faithful disciples take up the challenge, surrender to God's care, and know they will be fruitful because God is with them.

If we proclaim the Gospel, there will be opposition and persecution. For the vast majority of us this doesn't mean censorship or physical hardship. It does mean that we must set aside our own desires and preferences in order to surrender to the good of others. Concretely, this might mean reaching out to the one who has wronged or denounced us even when he or she has admitted no wrongdoing. It might mean the teen withstanding peer pressure to do something wrong. It might mean speaking the truth in a difficult situation or cleaning up one's language. Living liturgy means choosing the world of light—the world offered by Jesus—and living it, no matter what the cost.

✦ My ministry nurtures others to remain faithful to the Gospel in the midst of the cares and challenges of daily living whenever I . . .

Brief Silence

Prayer

O God, you bestow upon us dignity by your care for us. Help us to recognize our own worth and to grow in our ability to announce your presence to others by the goodness of our lives. We ask this through Christ our Lord. **Amen**.

SS. PETER AND PAUL, APOSTLES

Saints Peter and Paul were the two great apostles who preached to the Jews and Gentiles and received the martyr's crown. Let us reflect on how faithful we have been to living the Gospel and ask God to be our strength and courage . . .

Prayer
O God, you bless us with Saints Peter and Paul as models of good followers of Jesus. Be with us each day as we try to live the Gospel and make your Son Jesus Christ known to all those we meet. We ask this through Christ our Lord. **Amen.**

Gospel (Matt 16:13-19)
When Jesus went into the region of Caesarea Philippi he asked his disciples, "Who do people say that the Son of Man is?" They replied, "Some say John the Baptist, others Elijah, still others Jeremiah or one of the prophets." He said to them, "But who do you say that I am?" Simon Peter said in reply, "You are the Christ, the Son of the living God." Jesus said to him in reply, "Blessed are you, Simon son of Jonah. For flesh and blood has not revealed this to you, but my heavenly Father. And so I say to you, you are Peter, and upon this rock I will build my Church, and the gates of the netherworld shall not prevail against it. I will give you the keys to the Kingdom of heaven. Whatever you bind on earth shall be bound in heaven; and whatever you loose on earth shall be loosed in heaven."

Brief Silence

For Reflection

In the gospel Peter confesses Jesus as the Messiah, and Jesus establishes Peter as the rock upon which he would build his church. Here is the key to faithful discipleship: knowing and confessing Jesus. Without a personal relationship with Jesus, we cannot remain faithful to our mission. Nonetheless, the victory in which we share has its cost for us, just as it had for Jesus and for Peter and Paul. We will probably not be crucified (like Jesus and Peter) or beheaded (like Paul), but the self-giving that led to their faithfulness is the same self-giving to which we are called.

Repeated imprisonment didn't silence Peter or Paul; both preached the good news of salvation in Christ until their final suffering and death. Both were able to do so because Christ stood by them and gave them strength. So it is for us. Christ strengthens us to preach boldly and faithfully. Such living will bring us also to receive the "crown of righteousness." This is the victory that we celebrate this day. We may not proclaim Christ in great speeches, as did Peter and Paul. But we do proclaim Christ every day by the way we live. Self-giving and surrendering ourselves to God's will bring us the same victory shared by Peter and Paul.

✦ I am most aware that my self-giving in ministry and daily living is bringing me to the same victory shared by Peter and Paul when . . .

Brief Silence

Prayer

Lord God, you established your church on the two great pillars, Peter and Paul. Help us to have their strength and to witness to the Gospel with their fidelity. We ask this through Christ our Lord. **Amen.**

FOURTEENTH SUNDAY IN ORDINARY TIME

In this Sunday's gospel Jesus invites us to come to him. Let us ready our hearts once again to encounter Jesus who is meek and humble of heart. . .

Prayer

Gracious Father, you invite us to come to you for rest. Ease our burdens and lighten our hearts, that we might always follow your will faithfully. We ask this through Christ our Lord. **Amen**.

Gospel **(Matt 11:25-30)**

At that time Jesus exclaimed: "I give praise to you, Father, Lord of heaven and earth, for although you have hidden these things from the wise and the learned you have revealed them to little ones. Yes, Father, such has been your gracious will. All things have been handed over to me by my Father. No one knows the Son except the Father, and no one knows the Father except the Son and anyone to whom the Son wishes to reveal him.

"Come to me, all you who labor and are burdened, and I will give you rest. Take my yoke upon you and learn from me, for I am meek and humble of heart; and you will find rest for yourselves. For my yoke is easy, and my burden light."

Brief Silence

For Reflection

In this gospel Jesus pours out his "meek and humble" heart in love both for the Father and for his disciples. He praises God for graciously willing "little ones" to be the recipients of revelation. He calls disciples to himself that he might offer them deserved rest from their burdens. When we experience discipleship as hard, difficult, and challenging—as it is—we can find comfort and solace in the tender Christ who lightens our burdens. Although the Father and Jesus know each other intimately and are one with each other, Jesus still identifies so readily with the weaknesses and burdens of the human condition. All he asks is that we do as he did—surrender to doing the Father's "gracious will" and come to him. He is always there for us, giving us rest and refreshment.

Faithful discipleship calls for a self-sacrificing love that knows no bounds when the good of the other is at stake. No bounds—not even one's life. Faithful discipleship requires of us no less than dying to ourselves. We must let go of all our pretensions, become meek and humble like Jesus—become little ones—and serve others. In everyday terms this means that we always seek God's will in our lives.

✦ Through my ministry, I have come to know Jesus as "meek and humble of heart" by . . .

Brief Silence

Prayer

Gentle God, you care for us and call us to rest. Strengthen us for our ministry of bringing Christ's Body and Blood to those who hunger, and help us touch them with your promise of rest. We ask this through Christ our Lord. **Amen.**

FIFTEENTH SUNDAY IN ORDINARY TIME

God's word comes to us in many ways to bear fruit in our lives. Let us prepare our hearts to hear God's word through the ordinary circumstances of our lives . . .

Prayer
God of mystery, you reveal yourself to us through word and sacrament. Help us to listen to and understand all Jesus has taught us, so that our lives might reflect your goodness. We ask this through Christ our Lord. **Amen.**

Gospel (Matt 13:1-9 [Longer Form: Matt 13:1-23])

On that day, Jesus went out of the house and sat down by the sea. Such large crowds gathered around him that he got into a boat and sat down, and the whole crowd stood along the shore. And he spoke to them at length in parables, saying: "A sower went out to sow. And as he sowed, some seed fell on the path, and birds came and ate it up. Some fell on rocky ground, where it had little soil. It sprang up at once because the soil was not deep, and when the sun rose it was scorched, and it withered for lack of roots. Some seed fell among thorns, and the thorns grew up and choked it. But some seed fell on rich soil and produced fruit, a hundred or sixty or thirtyfold. Whoever has ears ought to hear."

Brief Silence

For Reflection

The images of this parable include sower, seed, and soil. If we see ourselves as the sower, the parable takes us in the direction of learning to know God and having union with God. We ourselves are the ones who spread the word of good news. This is discipleship! If we see ourselves as the seed, it reminds us that we sow God's word wherever we are, by word and example. This is discipleship! If we see ourselves as the soil (which is the tendency), we are directed to examine the cares and distractions of our lives to see if they stand in the way of open eyes and ears and hearts. Thus the parable touches our lives in terms of knowing God and doing as God wills, being faithful disciples, and being fertile so God's word can be fruitful.

The closer we come to Jesus the more layers of interpretation are opened up; the less we know Jesus, the more obscure is the parable or the more literal will be our interpretation. But most of all, we want to live our lives confident of the outcome, "achieving the end" God intended. We want to both *be* an abundant harvest as well as help to bring it about.

✦ I "sow" the Eucharist in others when I . . .

Brief Silence

Prayer

Patient God, you give us all we need to produce an abundant harvest. Strengthen us to minister with joy and abandon, sowing the seeds of your love. We ask this through Christ our Lord. **Amen**.

SIXTEENTH SUNDAY IN ORDINARY TIME

God is merciful and kind to all of us. Let us open our hearts to hear God's word and wait patiently for an abundant harvest . . .

Prayer

God our sovereign Lord, you sent your Son to live among us and announce to us that your reign is at hand. Be with us as we continue Jesus' saving ministry, that your kingdom might come. We ask this through Christ our Lord. **Amen.**

Gospel (Matt 13:24-30 [Longer Form: Matt 13:24-43])

Jesus proposed another parable to the crowds, saying: "The kingdom of heaven may be likened to a man who sowed good seed in his field. While everyone was asleep his enemy came and sowed weeds all through the wheat, and then went off. When the crop grew and bore fruit, the weeds appeared as well. The slaves of the householder came to him and said, 'Master, did you not sow good seed in your field? Where have the weeds come from?' He answered, 'An enemy has done this.' His slaves said to him, 'Do you want us to go and pull them up?' He replied, 'No, if you pull up the weeds you might uproot the wheat along with them. Let them grow together until harvest; then at harvest time I will say to the harvesters, "First collect the weeds and tie them in bundles for burning; but gather the wheat into my barn."'"

Brief Silence

For Reflection

What is the good news here for our daily living? True, some of us have a tendency to live in fear of God's judgment; we might think of ourselves only as weeds to be burned. We forget that, to be sure, in our daily living there will be times when we fall short of the demands of the gospel. But the rhythm of the paschal mystery—dying always leads to rising—invites us to look beyond the immediate moment, see the possibilities for repentance in our lives, trust in God's leniency and mercy, and be open to God's loving kindness. The weeds will grow. But God is patient. If we remember that the seed grows and leaven makes the dough rise, we are assured that death leads to life. This is paschal mystery living at its best.

Another consideration, of course, is that some have such a lax conscience that God's judgment is not something they think about or are concerned about. These folks need to recall the gospel exhortation: "Whoever has ears ought to hear." There is always time and need for repentance! This is why it is such good news that we hear this Sunday: God is kind and merciful, and patient beyond expectation.

✦ Some of the ways that I nurture the people closest to me whom I love are . . . This helps to bring about God's reign because . . .

Brief Silence

Prayer

O God, you sow the Good News of your saving deeds in our hearts. Strengthen us to be leaven in our world, so that your kingdom of peace and mercy may be fully established. We ask this through Christ our Lord.
Amen.

SEVENTEENTH SUNDAY IN ORDINARY TIME

We remember and celebrate the great gift God has given us in Christ. He is our great treasure, our pearl of great price. Let us reflect on how diligently we have searched for God . . .

Prayer

God of wisdom and understanding, you plant in our hearts the desire to search diligently for what we value most. Guide us in right ways, that we might one day enjoy the great treasure of everlasting life with you. We ask this through Christ our Lord. **Amen.**

Gospel **(Matt 13:44-52 or 13:44-46)**

Jesus said to his disciples: "The kingdom of heaven is like a treasure buried in a field, which a person finds and hides again, and out of joy goes and sells all that he has and buys that field. Again, the kingdom of heaven is like a merchant searching for fine pearls. When he finds a pearl of great price, he goes and sells all that he has and buys it. Again, the kingdom of heaven is like a net thrown into the sea, which collects fish of every kind. When it is full they haul it ashore and sit down to put what is good into buckets. What is bad they throw away. Thus it will be at the end of the age. The angels will go out and separate the wicked from the righteous and throw them into the fiery furnace, where there will be wailing and grinding of teeth.

"Do you understand all these things?" They answered, "Yes." And he replied, "Then every scribe who has been instructed in the kingdom of heaven is like the head of a household who brings from his storeroom both the new and the old."

Brief Silence

For Reflection

This Sunday's gospel includes three more short parables about the kingdom of God. So often these parables about God's kingdom take us to the end times and judgment—as illustrated in the first two parables by selling all to buy the field or the pearl of great price, and in the third parable by separating the good and bad fish. A judgment motif gives us a partial insight into what God's kingdom is: his everlasting and just reign and presence. Thus, God's kingdom is not a place or territory, but an exercise of God's dominion and will over all of creation.

It is sometimes difficult to keep our sight on what is our true treasure—being faithful disciples helping to make present God's reign. Living the Gospel is less something we actually "search" for and more something we live by, responding to the great value we have already been given. If we are aware of our own dignity as members of the Body of Christ (given at baptism), then we can more easily treasure and uphold the dignity of others. If we are aware of the abundance of risen life already given us, then we can work in justice and peace to help others share in the goodness of that same life. If we are aware of . . .

✦ When I search my heart, the thing of great value I find there is . . .

Brief Silence

Prayer

O God, you offer us a great treasure—eternal life with you. Help us to live our lives with discerning hearts, to find our truest treasure, and never to waver in our search for goodness and mercy. We ask this through Christ our Lord. **Amen.**

EIGHTEENTH SUNDAY IN ORDINARY TIME

In the gospel Jesus goes off to a deserted place to be by himself. Let us go off to a deserted place and ponder the care and goodness of God . . .

Prayer

Lavish God, you fill us with all good things. We bring to you grateful hearts, and ask that you open our hearts to give generously to those less fortunate than ourselves. We ask this through Christ our Lord. **Amen.**

Gospel (Matt 14:13-21)

When Jesus heard of the death of John the Baptist, he withdrew in a boat to a deserted place by himself. The crowds heard of this and followed him on foot from their towns. When he disembarked and saw the vast crowd, his heart was moved with pity for them, and he cured their sick. When it was evening, the disciples approached him and said, "This is a deserted place and it is already late; dismiss the crowds so that they can go to the villages and buy food for themselves." Jesus said to them, "There is no need for them to go away; give them some food yourselves." But they said to him, "Five loaves and two fish are all we have here." Then he said, "Bring them here to me," and he ordered the crowds to sit down on the grass. Taking the five loaves and the two fish, and looking up to heaven, he said the blessing, broke the loaves, and gave them to the disciples, who in turn gave them to the crowds. They all ate and were satisfied, and they picked up the fragments left over—twelve wicker baskets full. Those who ate were about five thousand men, not counting women and children.

Brief Silence

For Reflection

How human: Jesus is grieving the death of his cousin John! When the crowds go out to meet Jesus, however, they are not concerned about *his* need; instead, it is Jesus whose heart is filled with pity for *their* needs. The crowds approach Jesus and "his heart was moved with pity for them." Even in this most private of moments, Jesus finds the inner strength to reach out to others in need—"he cured their sick." Here is a sign of the kingdom: not that we ourselves have the power to cure the sick as Jesus did, but that we have the capacity and inner strength (helped by the Spirit who dwells within us) to reach out of ourselves for the sake of another.

Jesus compassionately and willingly meets the crowd's needs and does so with superabundance: he cures their sick, he feeds them with loaves and fish, and he does so with "twelve wicker baskets" left over. The abundance of the food is a measure of his abundant compassion. The real good news in this Sunday's gospel doesn't lie in the miracle in which the crowd's hunger is satisfied and Jesus proves his power. As wondrous as all this may be, even more wondrous still is its significance: the abundant food freely given marks this as a sure sign that in the person of Jesus the kingdom of God has appeared.

✦ Some ways that my daily living of the Eucharist satisfies the hungers of those around me are . . .

Brief Silence

Prayer

O God, you nourish us abundantly and care for all our needs. Help us to recognize all you give us, to have grateful hearts, and to open our own hearts to the needs of others. We ask this through Christ our Lord. **Amen.**

NINETEENTH SUNDAY IN ORDINARY TIME

In the gospel this Sunday Jesus has the power to calm the stormy sea and save Peter from drowning. Let us open our hearts to the saving power of Jesus . . .

Prayer

Almighty God, you created all things and have power over them. When we are in trouble, help us to cry "Lord, save me!" and always be confident that you are at our side. We ask this through Christ our Lord. **Amen.**

Gospel (Matt 14:22-33)

After he had fed the people, Jesus made the disciples get into a boat and precede him to the other side, while he dismissed the crowds. After doing so, he went up on the mountain by himself to pray. When it was evening he was there alone. Meanwhile the boat, already a few miles offshore, was being tossed about by the waves, for the wind was against it. During the fourth watch of the night, he came toward them walking on the sea. When the disciples saw him walking on the sea they were terrified. "It is a ghost," they said, and they cried out in fear. At once Jesus spoke to them, "Take courage, it is I; do not be afraid." Peter said to him in reply, "Lord, if it is you, command me to come to you on the water." He said, "Come." Peter got out of the boat and began to walk on the water toward Jesus. But when he saw how strong the wind was he became frightened; and, beginning to sink, he cried out, "Lord, save me!" Immediately Jesus stretched out his hand and caught Peter, and said to him, "O you of little faith, why did you doubt?" After they got into the boat, the wind died down. Those who were in the boat did him homage, saying, "Truly, you are the Son of God."

Brief Silence

For Reflection

Jesus is truly the presence of God among us ("Son of God"), revealing what nature can never fully manifest: God acting to save. The greatest power of God is not revealed in the might of nature (wind, earthquake, fire—first reading; strong wind, tossed about by waves—gospel), but in God's saving us ("Lord, save me!"). Jesus' simple command to Peter, "Come," is also a command to us—and, like Peter, it is what saves us too. Jesus' command to "Come" is also the command to become his disciples.

Our discipleship is not only about continuing Jesus' saving work. Discipleship is also about our fulfilling the command Jesus gives to all: to come to him and be saved. Indeed, in the very coming to Jesus for salvation we are exercising the basic work of discipleship: furthering the kingdom of God, a reign in which all are one with Jesus and the Father through the power of the Holy Spirit. We usually think of discipleship as reaching out to others, and it surely is that. This Sunday's gospel, however, opens up for us another and prior dimension of discipleship—we must reach out to Jesus and be grasped by his saving hand. By this utter intimacy of relationship—reaching out, touching, being saved—are we in a unique relationship with Jesus, a relationship that enables us to be his risen presence in our world and carry forward his saving mission.

✦ My ministry embodies God's salvation for those "tossed about by the waves" of life whenever I . . .

Brief Silence

Prayer

Lord God, you grasp us and save us when we reach out to you. Help us to be faithful to those who reach out to us for help, as you have been faithful to us. Increase our faith, that we might look only to you for our help and salvation. We ask this through Christ our Lord. **Amen.**

ASSUMPTION OF THE BLESSED VIRGIN MARY

Today we celebrate Mary who has been taken up into heavenly glory. Let us turn to her in prayer and ask for her intercession, so that one day we too will share in everlasting glory . . .

Prayer

Saving God, you took Mary into heaven, body and soul, preserving her body whole and spotless. Through her intercession may we too one day join you in everlasting life. We ask this through Christ our Lord. **Amen.**

Gospel (Luke 1:39-56)

Mary set out and traveled to the hill country in haste to a town of Judah, where she entered the house of Zechariah and greeted Elizabeth. When Elizabeth heard Mary's greeting, the infant leaped in her womb, and Elizabeth, filled with the Holy Spirit, cried out in a loud voice and said, "Blessed are you among women, and blessed is the fruit of your womb. And how does this happen to me, that the mother of my Lord should come to me? For at the moment the sound of your greeting reached my ears, the infant in my womb leaped for joy. Blessed are you who believed that what was spoken to you by the Lord would be fulfilled."

And Mary said: / "My soul proclaims the greatness of the Lord; / my spirit rejoices in God my Savior / for he has looked upon his lowly servant. / From this day all generations will call me blessed: / the Almighty has done great things for me, / and holy is his Name. / He has mercy on those who fear him / in every generation. / He has shown the strength of his arm, / and has scattered the proud in their conceit. / He has cast down the mighty from their thrones, / and has lifted up the lowly. / He has filled the hungry with good things, / and the rich he has sent away empty. / He has come to the help of his servant Israel /

for he has remembered his promise of mercy, / the promise he made to our fathers, / to Abraham and his children forever."

Mary remained with her about three months and then returned to her home.

Brief Silence

For Reflection

The significance of the gospel for us is that Mary has gone before us and, united with her Son in eternity, awaits our entry into the same eschatological glory. This solemnity is about beginning times and end times; it looks both backward and forward—backward to Mary's assumption into heaven and forward to the glory that awaits all who are faithful to Christ. The God who "lifted up his lowly servant," Mary, will lift up all who, like Mary, have believed in God's word and fulfilled God's will.

Each day at the church's evening prayer we sing together Mary's great song of praise, the *Magnificat*. In so doing we align ourselves with Mary and all she did. Like her, we are the lowly on whom God showers many blessings. Like Mary, we must be lowly ones who do God's will. Like Mary, our discipleship must be of humble service, putting others' needs before our own. Sometimes Mary is presented as the model disciple, but she may seem far beyond us. This gospel shows us the simple, everyday side of Mary. She did what women forever have done . . . helped each other at childbearing time. She shows all of us—women and men, mothers and childless—that greatness is achieved by giving generously without counting the cost in the little things.

✦ The glory that awaits those who are faithful to God's word impacts how I live and do my ministry in that . . .

Brief Silence

Prayer

God of glory, you are worthy of all praise for you have done great things for us. Help us to be like Mary in her fidelity to your will, and to live our discipleship in such a way that it honors you always. We ask this through Christ our Lord. **Amen.**

TWENTIETH SUNDAY IN ORDINARY TIME

The Canaanite woman in this Sunday's gospel persists in begging Jesus to heal her daughter. We make her prayer our own as we ask Jesus to have mercy on us and heal us . . .

Prayer

Lord God, your divine Son brought healing to those who persisted in their requests. Help us to be persistent in our own prayer, confident that you give us all that we need. We ask this through Christ our Lord. **Amen.**

Gospel (Matt 15:21-28)

At that time, Jesus withdrew to the region of Tyre and Sidon. And behold, a Canaanite woman of that district came and called out, "Have pity on me, Lord, Son of David! My daughter is tormented by a demon." But Jesus did not say a word in answer to her. Jesus' disciples came and asked him, "Send her away, for she keeps calling out after us." He said in reply, "I was sent only to the lost sheep of the house of Israel." But the woman came and did Jesus homage, saying, "Lord, help me." He said in reply, "It is not right to take the food of the children and throw it to the dogs." She said, "Please, Lord, for even the dogs eat the scraps that fall from the table of their masters." Then Jesus said to her in reply, "O woman, great is your faith! Let it be done for you as you wish." And the woman's daughter was healed from that hour.

Brief Silence

For Reflection

All of us struggle with persistence. We get serious about losing weight but then give up when it doesn't come off fast enough or we reach a plateau. Our doctor recommends exercise, and we do so for a few days after the doctor visit and then go back to life as usual. Just as difficult (perhaps even more so!) is persistence in prayer, in good works, or with any spiritual discipline. The gospel woman reminds us that sometimes the sheer persistence can be the prayer, the good work, the spiritual discipline. Sometimes sheer persistence brings us to the great faith that establishes the intimate relationship with Jesus, bringing salvation to all who seek him.

The woman approaches Jesus, but she is not initially welcomed. Still she persists in her request. She is absolutely single-minded. In this the woman in the gospel demonstrates something significant about faith: sheer persistence matters. Although rebuffed by disciples and ignored by Jesus, she persists with surprising results. Her dogged persistence is recognized by Jesus for what it truly is—great faith (the only person in Matthew's Gospel who is praised for great faith)—and Jesus does have pity on her. Rather than being sent away without her request fulfilled, the woman's faith moves Jesus to grant her request: "the woman's daughter was healed."

✦ Eucharist includes my cry of pity for others whenever I . . .

Brief Silence

Prayer

Healing God, you care for us and listen to our cries for help. Heal us of all that leads us to stray from you, bring us to deep faith, and help us to care for others. We ask this through Christ our Lord. **Amen.**

TWENTY-FIRST SUNDAY IN ORDINARY TIME

Because of God's gift of revelation, Peter is able to acknowledge Jesus as the Christ. Let us open ourselves to Jesus' presence among us and acknowledge that he is the Christ, our Savior . . .

Prayer

Lord God, you sent your Son Jesus to dwell among us, "the Son of the living God." Help us to grow in our own dignity as your beloved sons and daughters. We ask this through Christ our Lord. **Amen.**

Gospel (Matt 16:13-20)

Jesus went into the region of Caesarea Philippi and he asked his disciples, "Who do people say that the Son of Man is?" They replied, "Some say John the Baptist, others Elijah, still others Jeremiah or one of the prophets." He said to them, "But who do you say that I am?" Simon Peter said in reply, "You are the Christ, the Son of the living God." Jesus said to him in reply, "Blessed are you, Simon son of Jonah. For flesh and blood has not revealed this to you, but my heavenly Father. And so I say to you, you are Peter, and upon this rock I will build my church, and the gates of the netherworld shall not prevail against it. I will give you the keys to the kingdom of heaven. Whatever you bind on earth shall be bound in heaven; and whatever you loose on earth shall be loosed in heaven." Then he strictly ordered his disciples to tell no one that he was the Christ.

Brief Silence

For Reflection

This is, indeed, a gospel of "gifts"! Peter does not recognize Jesus as "the Christ, the Son of the living God" by his own insight, but because God has revealed it to him. Only by God's gift is Peter able to make his profession of faith and receive his role of leadership. Further, Jesus gives his disciples the gift of the church as well as the gift of leadership to guide it faithfully. Revelation, faith, church, leadership—gift upon gift!

Just as it was with Peter, we ourselves can recognize Jesus because God has revealed him to us. The challenge of this Sunday's gospel, then, is to be as attentive to Jesus' presence and identity as was Peter and to recognize that our own discipleship is a gracious gift of God. One aspect of discipleship is that we manifest by our own good works the baptismal identity that has been bestowed on us: to be the Body of Christ in our world, to be the presence of the risen Christ to others, to announce that salvation has dawned upon us, to be rocks upon which the church continues to grow and be strengthened. That Jesus is the Son of Man, the Son of the living God, the Christ, the long-awaited Messiah is a truth which has to be revealed. Once such revelation has been truly heard and believed, nothing can prevail against the church.

✦ Jesus has been revealed to me as the "Christ, the Son of the living God" by . . .

Brief Silence

Prayer

Lord God, you reveal yourself to us in your care and love for us. Help us to recognize your presence in others and to care for and love them as you do. We ask this through Christ our Lord. **Amen**.

TWENTY-SECOND SUNDAY IN ORDINARY TIME

In this Sunday's gospel Jesus tells his disciples that he must go to Jerusalem to suffer, die, and be raised up. Let us prepare to walk to Jerusalem with Jesus and share in his dying and rising . . .

Prayer

Almighty God, by raising your Son to risen life you give us a share in that same life. Help us to be faithful to the grace you have given us to continue Jesus' saving mission. We ask this through Christ our Lord. **Amen.**

Gospel (Matt 16:21-27)

Jesus began to show his disciples that he must go to Jerusalem and suffer greatly from the elders, the chief priests, and the scribes, and be killed and on the third day be raised. Then Peter took Jesus aside and began to rebuke him, "God forbid, Lord! No such thing shall ever happen to you." He turned and said to Peter, "Get behind me, Satan! You are an obstacle to me. You are thinking not as God does, but as human beings do."

Then Jesus said to his disciples, "Whoever wishes to come after me must deny himself, take up his cross, and follow me. For whoever wishes to save his life will lose it, but whoever loses his life for my sake will find it. What profit would there be for one to gain the whole world and forfeit his life? Or what can one give in exchange for his life? For the Son of Man will come with his angels in his Father's glory, and then he will repay all according to his conduct."

Brief Silence

AUGUST 31, 2008

For Reflection

Suffering is something we simply cannot avoid because it takes us beyond the limits of human resilience, the threshold of pain, or our emotional self-control and stability. People sometimes rationalize suffering as something-gone-wrong, as the absence of God, or as being punished by God. In light of the cross and resurrection, however, suffering can become a more intense experience of God's presence and God's promise. This Sunday's gospel starkly tells us that the only way to life is through death, through suffering.

Regardless of Peter's good intentions to protect his Master and Lord, Jesus turns Peter's objection to suffering into the profound meaning of virtually everything Jesus is about, caught in a few pithy sayings: Jesus' followers must deny themselves and take up his cross; the followers must let go of their life (self-will, human responses, human way of thinking) in order to find life; unless one dies one cannot rise. Jesus forthrightly reveals to his disciples what awaits—death, but also resurrection. If we want to go where Jesus ultimately went—to glory—there is only one road: to Jerusalem where death awaits. The human response is to recoil (Peter); the divine call is to take up the cross. Jesus does not expect of us any suffering he himself has not endured; Jesus shares with us the glory he himself is given. This is good news, indeed!

✦ I become Christ's food for others on their journey to Jerusalem when I . . .

Brief Silence

Prayer

Almighty God, you raised your Son to new life. Help us to embrace dying to self, thus uniting ourselves with Christ's suffering and death, so that we might one day share everlasting life with him. We ask this through Christ our Lord. **Amen.**

TWENTY-THIRD SUNDAY IN ORDINARY TIME

In the gospel this Sunday, Jesus lays before us perhaps one of the most difficult challenges of being members of the Christian community—healing relationships that are broken. We pause now to acknowledge before God our need for healing and reconciliation in our families, workplaces, and church . . .

Prayer

Heavenly Father, you reconcile those who have strayed from your loving embrace with mercy and compassion. Help us to reach out to those who have hurt us and bring healing to all our relationships. We ask this through Christ our Lord. **Amen.**

Gospel (Matt 18:15-20)

Jesus said to his disciples: "If your brother sins against you, go and tell him his fault between you and him alone. If he listens to you, you have won over your brother. If he does not listen, take one or two others along with you, so that 'every fact may be established on the testimony of two or three witnesses.' If he refuses to listen to them, tell the church. If he refuses to listen even to the church, then treat him as you would a Gentile or a tax collector. Amen, I say to you, whatever you bind on earth shall be bound in heaven, and whatever you loose on earth shall be loosed in heaven. Again, amen, I say to you, if two of you agree on earth about anything for which they are to pray, it shall be granted to them by my heavenly Father. For where two or three are gathered together in my name, there am I in the midst of them."

Brief Silence

For Reflection

In the gospel, Jesus teaches his disciples how to deal with conflicts and strife in the church. The challenge he lays down is the hard work of addressing rifts directly, honestly, repeatedly, and prayerfully. The desired outcome of the entire process is repentance and reconciliation. What is essentially at stake is not merely the healing of a personal rift but the very life of the church as a community. In this life we will never be a perfect community or a perfect church because we always have the human dimension at work, with its imperfections and weaknesses. Ultimately, when we act as church to reconcile, we are acting as the Body of Christ in consort with our Head, Christ himself. Reconciliation is essential in the church because of our very identity as the Body of Christ.

Some strong motivation usually has to be present in order for corrections to be given or received and true reconciliation to take place. The last line of this gospel gives us a clue as to what underlying motivation is really the strongest: "For where two or three are gathered together in my name, there am I in the midst of them." In other words, our strongest motivation urging us to charitable correction is the fact that we share a common identity as the Body of Christ. We ourselves aren't the reconcilers; it is the power of Christ acting through his Body.

✦ Eating and drinking at the eucharistic table challenges me to be reconciled with another because . . .

Brief Silence

Prayer

Merciful God, you sent your Son to reconcile us to you and with each other. Help us to be one in your divine Son, to ask for what we need, and to preserve the unity of the Body of Christ. We ask this through Christ our Lord. **Amen**.

EXALTATION OF THE HOLY CROSS

This Sunday we exalt the cross, the instrument of Christ's glory and our salvation. Let us reflect on and celebrate this great mystery . . .

Prayer

Exalted God, your Son died on the cross for our salvation. Help us to take up our own daily cross of dying to self, so that one day we might share in Jesus' everlasting glory. We ask this through Christ our Lord. **Amen.**

Gospel (John 3:13-17)

Jesus said to Nicodemus: "No one has gone up to heaven except the one who has come down from heaven, the Son of Man. And just as Moses lifted up the serpent in the desert, so must the Son of Man be lifted up, so that everyone who believes in him may have eternal life."

For God so loved the world that he gave his only Son, so that he who believes in him might not perish but might have eternal life. For God did not send his Son into the world to condemn the world, but that the world might be saved through him.

Brief Silence

SEPTEMBER 14, 2008

For Reflection

The depth of God's love for the world becomes fully revealed in the death of Jesus on the cross. Through the self-emptying obedience of Jesus, the cross, a sign of ignominy, becomes a sign of exaltation—not only of Jesus himself whom God lifts up in glory but also of all of us who gaze upon the cross in faith and are lifted up to eternal life. The challenge of this feast and its proper readings is to see through the cross to the eternal life that it promises. The way to this eternal life is through humble obedience and through believing in God's "only Son" (gospel). Obedience and belief are two sides of the same coin.

Both obedience and belief draw their efficacy by being in relationship with another. In terms of the cross, that "other" is Jesus himself. He is the model for our embracing the cross as both dying to self and rising to glory. Herein is the mystery: in dying to self, in self-emptying, we are more perfectly conformed to Christ. And this is the whole goal of our Christian life: conformity to Christ. Thus we can rightly say, in the very dying is the rising, in the self-emptying is the new life, in the suffering is the glory. That is why this day is rightly named the *Exaltation* of the Holy Cross.

✦ My ministry embodies how "God so loved the world" when . . .

Brief Silence

Prayer

Loving God, your Son was lifted up on the cross for our salvation. Help us to return your love for us, not only in our prayer and attentiveness to your presence, but also in our willingness to die to ourselves for the sake of others. We ask this through Christ our Lord. **Amen.**

TWENTY-FIFTH SUNDAY IN ORDINARY TIME

God offers us salvation freely and generously. Let us pause in our busy lives to open our hearts to such a generous God and ask for mercy . . .

Prayer

Generous God, you offer salvation to all those who seek it. Help us to appreciate your gift of love to us and to work diligently to make your ways known, no matter at what hour we are called. We ask this through Christ our Lord. **Amen.**

Gospel (Matt 20:1-16a)

Jesus told his disciples this parable: "The kingdom of heaven is like a landowner who went out at dawn to hire laborers for his vineyard. After agreeing with them for the usual daily wage, he sent them into his vineyard. Going out about nine o'clock, the landowner saw others standing idle in the marketplace, and he said to them, 'You too go into my vineyard, and I will give you what is just.' So they went off. And he went out again around noon, and around three o'clock, and did likewise. Going out about five o'clock, the landowner found others standing around, and said to them, 'Why do you stand here idle all day?' They answered, 'Because no one has hired us.' He said to them, 'You too go into my vineyard.' When it was evening the owner of the vineyard said to his foreman, 'Summon the laborers and give them their pay, beginning with the last and ending with the first.' When those who had started about five o'clock came, each received the usual daily wage. So when the first came, they thought that they would receive more, but each of them also got the usual wage. And on receiving it they grumbled against the landowner, saying, 'These last ones worked only one hour, and you have made them equal to us, who bore the day's burden and the heat.' He said to one of them in reply, 'My friend, I am not cheating you. Did you not agree with me for the

SEPTEMBER 21, 2008

usual daily wage? Take what is yours and go. What if I wish to give this last one the same as you? Or am I not free to do as I wish with my own money? Are you envious because I am generous?' Thus, the last will be first, and the first will be last."

Brief Silence

For Reflection

When hearing this gospel, we tend to focus on hours and wages: the laborers understand justice as prorated wages, equitable pay for the number of hours worked. However, this parable is really about God's ways (see first reading) and God's justice: what God is offering is not wages, but salvation, which is the same for everyone. The surprise of the parable is that salvation is not earned at all, but it is God's gift to us and God gives it generously. No matter at what hour we come, salvation is granted. All we need do is come!

We often put off to the eleventh hour some piece of work that we have to do with respect to God or each other (e.g., prayer, forgiveness, charity, justice, etc.). If this parable teaches us something about how great and generous God is, then we are called to this same greatness and generosity. Wouldn't nations be different if debts could be forgiven and those who have were generous to those who have not? Wouldn't families be different if hurtful behavior ceased and was forgiven generously? Wouldn't individuals be different if we measured another only by his or her goodness? The landowner says to his grumbling laborers, "Are you envious because I am generous?" God gives generously beyond what we deserve. God gives salvation.

✦ Some ways that I might extend to others the kind of generosity God demonstrates in the parable are . . .

Brief Silence

Prayer

God of salvation, you earnestly desire that we receive eternal life. Strengthen us to work faithfully in your vineyard and to receive graciously and with grateful hearts all the gifts you offer us. We ask this through Christ our Lord. **Amen.**

TWENTY-SIXTH SUNDAY IN ORDINARY TIME

God invites us to believe and change our lives so that we may enter God's kingdom. Let us ask for the grace of conversion and seek God's help so we can be faithful to our call . . .

Prayer

O God, you make your divine will known to us. Help us to be faithful to what you ask of us, and to live our lives with a willing spirit. We ask this through Christ our Lord. **Amen.**

Gospel **(Matt 21:28-32)**

Jesus said to the chief priests and elders of the people: "What is your opinion? A man had two sons. He came to the first and said, 'Son, go out and work in the vineyard today.' He said in reply, 'I will not,' but afterwards changed his mind and went. The man came to the other son and gave the same order. He said in reply, 'Yes, sir,' but did not go. Which of the two did his father's will?" They answered, "The first." Jesus said to them, "Amen, I say to you, tax collectors and prostitutes are entering the kingdom of God before you. When John came to you in the way of righteousness, you did not believe him; but tax collectors and prostitutes did. Yet even when you saw that, you did not later change your minds and believe him."

Brief Silence

SEPTEMBER 28, 2008

For Reflection

In the gospel, Jesus asks who is doing the "father's will." It is not the son with the right words, promises, or intentions; rather, it is the son who undergoes conversion of heart. Conversion may not always be instantaneous (first son), but its authenticity is revealed in action, as modeled by tax collectors and prostitutes who believed John's message and "are entering the kingdom of God." Because the tax collectors and prostitutes believed, they changed their lives. Similarly with us: we enter the kingdom of God when we believe and change our lives.

This gospel is a great example of the saying "actions speak louder than words." It is a reminder that belief isn't simply a matter of saying yes or professing creeds. Belief is action, follow-through. Those who believed John the Baptist changed their minds (that is, their lives) by repenting. Those who believe Jesus do the same. We Christians can choose to change our lives. It is the prerogative of Christians to change their minds (their lives). Let's do it! If tax collectors and prostitutes (symbols for great sinners) can enter the kingdom of God, then there's got to be great hope for all of us! Taking their lead, all we need to do is make *metanoia*—change—a permanent part of our spiritual life. Spirituality is about growth that can only come from the willingness to let go and change.

✦ Distributing the Body or Blood of Christ calls me to a deeper *yes* to God and God's people because . . . It calls me to change because . . .

Brief Silence

Prayer

Merciful God, you are compassionate and kind, and patient with us as we learn to change our ways to your ways. Be with us in our struggle to be faithful, and encourage us through your presence. We ask this through Christ our Lord. **Amen.**

TWENTY-SEVENTH SUNDAY IN ORDINARY TIME

God has planted the vineyard of the kingdom among us and calls us to bring it to fruition. Let us reflect on our life and ministry so that we can be faithful to God's call . . .

Prayer

Tender-loving God, you sent your Son among us to teach us your ways. Help us to listen to him and follow his way of obedience to you. We ask this through Christ our Lord. **Amen**.

Gospel **(Matt 21:33-43)**

Jesus said to the chief priests and the elders of the people: "Hear another parable. There was a landowner who planted a vineyard, put a hedge around it, dug a wine press in it, and built a tower. Then he leased it to tenants and went on a journey. When vintage time drew near, he sent his servants to the tenants to obtain his produce. But the tenants seized the servants and one they beat, another they killed, and a third they stoned. Again he sent other servants, more numerous than the first ones, but they treated them in the same way. Finally, he sent his son to them, thinking, 'They will respect my son.' But when the tenants saw the son, they said to one another, 'This is the heir. Come, let us kill him and acquire his inheritance.' They seized him, threw him out of the vineyard, and killed him. What will the owner of the vineyard do to those tenants when he comes?" They answered him, "He will put those wretched men to a wretched death and lease his vineyard to other tenants who will give him the produce at the proper times." Jesus said to them, "Did you never read in the Scriptures: / *The stone that the builders rejected / has become the cornerstone; / by the Lord has this been done, / and it is wonderful in our eyes?*

/ Therefore, I say to you, the kingdom of God will be taken away from you and given to a people that will produce its fruit."

Brief Silence

For Reflection

In Matthew the vineyard is not destroyed because the new vineyard is nurtured by God's own Son who abides in those who claim Jesus is Lord. New tenants are brought in so that the vineyard will produce good fruit. The initial tenants are thinking pretty fuzzily—if they kill the Son, they will inherit the kingdom. The irony in the story is that in killing the Son to take ownership of the vineyard themselves, they actually lose everything, even their own lives. For those new tenants who are faithful, they gain everything—the kingdom, eternal life.

The good news of this gospel is that the kingdom will survive no matter how the "tenants" act, because the cornerstone is Christ. This provides a metaphor for our own living. No matter in what shape the vineyard of our own lives is—whether we need pruning or we seem to be in a dry desert—if we keep our eyes on Christ as the cornerstone of our lives we will be fruitful, enjoy being tenants in God's kingdom, and not fear judgment. A message of judgment is often hard for us to hear. However, it is an essential aspect of the faithful proclamation of the Gospel and calls us to accountability for the way we live. All we need do is be faithful; God will take care of the rest.

✦ At Eucharist God sustains the divine vineyard in me by . . . at Eucharist I give to God the produce that God deserves by . . .

Brief Silence

Prayer

Gracious God, you care for those whom you have called to be your people. Help us to keep our eyes on Jesus as the cornerstone of our lives, and to be faithful to the ministry to which you have called us. We ask this through Christ our Lord. **Amen.**

TWENTY-EIGHTH SUNDAY IN ORDINARY TIME

God invites us to share in his messianic banquet each time we gather to celebrate Eucharist. Let us reflect on this lavish gift God has bestowed on us and express gratitude and praise to God for such goodness . . .

Prayer

Generous and gracious God, you spread a lavish banquet table before us and invite us constantly to share in your feast. Help us to respond to your invitation to love with open hearts. We ask this through Christ our Lord. **Amen.**

Gospel **(Matt 22:1-10 [Longer Form: Matt 22:1-14])**

Jesus again in reply spoke to the chief priests and elders of the people in parables, saying, "The kingdom of heaven may be likened to a king who gave a wedding feast for his son. He dispatched his servants to summon the invited guests to the feast, but they refused to come. A second time he sent other servants, saying, 'Tell those invited: "Behold, I have prepared my banquet, my calves and fattened cattle are killed, and everything is ready; come to the feast."' Some ignored the invitation and went away, one to his farm, another to his business. The rest laid hold of his servants, mistreated them, and killed them. The king was enraged and sent his troops, destroyed those murderers, and burned their city. Then he said to his servants, 'The feast is ready, but those who were invited were not worthy to come. Go out, therefore, into the main roads and invite to the feast whomever you find.' The servants went out into the streets and gathered all they found, bad and good alike, and the hall was filled with guests."

Brief Silence

OCTOBER 12, 2008

For Reflection

In Jesus' parable, the invitation issued is extraordinary: it comes from a king, it involves a lavish feast for the wedding of his son, it is issued several times. Who could refuse it? Yet, people foolishly do and with tragic consequences. But in fact, even more is at stake for us than a royal dinner. The wedding feast is to be nothing less than the messianic banquet of eternal life. This is the invitation that is issued to us; our response is either to receive or reject eternal life. This is what is at stake in accepting the invitation: eternal life.

Our response, however, must be more than a matter of merely coming to the banquet. The last part of the gospel includes a judgment: just as the king made the banquet ready by preparing it, the guests must prepare for the banquet as well ("dressed in a wedding garment"). All peoples are invited to God's banquet, but there are responsibilities that accompany the invitation. Sinners are invited ("invite . . . whomever you find . . . bad and good alike"), but they must repent of their sinful ways and live good lives. To share in God's banquet we must do our part. We must live our lives doing God's will. We must be faithful subjects of our divine King by being faithful disciples of the King's Son.

✦ My daily living summons others to God's heavenly banquet when I . . .

Brief Silence

Prayer

O loving God, you provide us with all good things. Help us to prepare well to share at your banquet in this life and to enjoy the heavenly banquet forever. We ask this through Christ our Lord. **Amen.**

TWENTY-NINTH SUNDAY IN ORDINARY TIME

In the gospel this Sunday Jesus invites us to give to God what belongs to God. Let us ask for the strength to surrender ourselves to God . . .

Prayer

Lord our God, you invite us to pay our due to both our earthly kingdom and to your heavenly kingdom. Help us to live in justice and truth, giving to all their just share. We ask this through Christ our Lord. **Amen.**

Gospel (Matt 22:15-21)

The Pharisees went off and plotted how they might entrap Jesus in speech. They sent their disciples to him, with the Herodians, saying, "Teacher, we know that you are a truthful man and that you teach the way of God in accordance with the truth. And you are not concerned with anyone's opinion, for you do not regard a person's status. Tell us, then, what is your opinion: Is it lawful to pay the census tax to Caesar or not?" Knowing their malice, Jesus said, "Why are you testing me, you hypocrites? Show me the coin that pays the census tax." Then they handed him the Roman coin. He said to them, "Whose image is this and whose inscription?" They replied, "Caesar's." At that he said to them, "Then repay to Caesar what belongs to Caesar and to God what belongs to God."

Brief Silence

OCTOBER 19, 2008

For Reflection

The context for this Sunday's gospel is the escalating conflict between Jesus and the Jewish authorities, a conflict that leads to Jesus' passion and death. The leading Jews are overtly plotting how they might "entrap Jesus in speech." They begin their offensive rather sarcastically ("Teacher, we know that you are a truthful man . . ."). Ironically, it is precisely in their sarcasm that they speak the greatest truth: instead of shying away from the confrontation or defusing it, Jesus is unwaveringly truthful; he addresses the conflict head on. He has clarity about what is central—God and the kingdom—and so he is able to give to God what belongs to God: his very self. Discipleship requires of us nothing less. Would that we have the clarity about our life and duties as Jesus portrays in the gospel! Yet, if we keep our focus on Jesus, this does bring a clarity to us.

"Dualism" claims God is in one sphere (heaven) and everything else is in another (this world) and that these spheres are mutually exclusive. Jesus challenges this dualism, however, and asserts that a right perspective means that we understand God as sovereign in all spheres, but that other spheres might have their justifiable claim on us. Christian living is being comfortable in all spheres, all having their just claim on us, without compromising God's sovereignty.

✦ I demonstrate that "what belongs to God" is more important to me than "what belongs to Caesar" by . . .

Brief Silence

Prayer

Almighty God, you are sovereign over all creation. Help us to be clear about where our truest allegiance is, and to be faithful to all you ask of us. We ask this through Christ our Lord. **Amen.**

THIRTIETH SUNDAY IN ORDINARY TIME

In this Sunday's gospel Jesus reminds us that everything can be summed up in loving God with our whole hearts, souls, and minds and loving our neighbor as ourselves. We ask God's pardon for our failures to love, and we pray for the strength to love more generously . . .

Prayer

God of life and love, you teach us how to live and give us clear commandments to guide us. Help us to love more perfectly, that we might always obey your laws. We ask this through Christ our Lord. **Amen.**

Gospel (Matt 22:34-40)

When the Pharisees heard that Jesus had silenced the Sadducees, they gathered together, and one of them, a scholar of the law, tested him by asking, "Teacher, which commandment in the law is the greatest?" He said to him, "You shall love the Lord, your God, with all your heart, with all your soul, and with all your mind. This is the greatest and the first commandment. The second is like it: You shall love your neighbor as yourself. The whole law and the prophets depend on these two commandments."

Brief Silence

For Reflection

Sometimes we compartmentalize our lives in such a way that we express our love of God only in terms of religious practices, for example, faithfully going to Sunday Mass, saying prayers, etc. Genuine love of God must also be expressed in care for widows, the orphan, the poor—indeed, all our neighbors. Thus, Jesus' words in this gospel aren't empty ones, for sure. He tells the Pharisees that they must love with their all. This is exactly what Jesus did—he loved with his all to the extent that he gave his life for us. Like Jesus, we demonstrate loving God with our all by wholeheartedly giving to others. Love makes its demands on us.

Our love of God by loving neighbor in this life is a kind of "practice" for the life of fulfillment and total loving that will be ours as we share eternally in the messianic banquet. It is this promise of sharing in the messianic banquet that strengthens us to be self-giving as Jesus was. This is how we daily love our neighbor: by being self-giving in all we do, by caring for the good of others, by treating everyone we meet as if he or she were our neighbor. Thus, Jesus' commandment to love is truly inclusive, moving us beyond the close circle we naturally love.

✦ My love of Christ in the Eucharist *requires* me to love the Christ found in my neighbor because . . .

Brief Silence

Prayer

Loving God, you are the perfection of love. Strengthen us to love others and to witness to them your care and love for us. We ask this through Christ our Lord. **Amen.**

ALL SAINTS

This day we honor the saints in heaven. Let us reflect on our own daily living to see how we might grow in holiness . . .

Prayer

Holy God, you are worthy of all praise and blessing. Be with us as we strive to grow in holiness, and help us one day to share in your everlasting life with the saints in heaven. We ask this through Christ our Lord. **Amen**.

Gospel **(Matt 5:1-12a)**

When Jesus saw the crowds, he went up the mountain, and after he had sat down, his disciples came to him. He began to teach them, saying: / "Blessed are the poor in spirit, / for theirs is the Kingdom of heaven. / Blessed are they who mourn, / for they will be comforted. / Blessed are the meek, / for they will inherit the land. / Blessed are they who hunger and thirst for righteousness, / for they will be satisfied. / Blessed are the merciful, / for they will be shown mercy. / Blessed are the clean of heart, / for they will see God. / Blessed are the peacemakers, / for they will be called children of God. / Blessed are they who are persecuted for the sake of righteousness, / for theirs is the Kingdom of heaven. / Blessed are you when they insult you and persecute you and utter every kind of evil against you falsely because of me. Rejoice and be glad, for your reward will be great in heaven."

Brief Silence

For Reflection

We've been journeying through Ordinary Time for a good number of weeks now (ever since Pentecost back in May), and the journey is heating up. Jesus is in Jerusalem and the conflict between him and the Jewish authorities is coming to a head. "We interrupt this important journey to bring you an important announcement . . ." This is what the solemnity of All Saints is all about—this journey leads somewhere, and not just to Jerusalem. This solemnity reminds us that the journey is worthwhile because it helps us to have a long-range vision of what happens at the end of the journey for faithful disciples.

We disciples pass through Jerusalem (and death) to get where we really want to go—to the messianic banquet, to eternal life. Nearing the end of the liturgical year when our focus shifts to the end times, this solemnity does double duty. It both celebrates those faithful disciples (saints) who enjoy their "reward . . . in heaven" and signals the fullness of glory that still awaits us. The saints' victory encourages our fidelity. Their glory strengthens our resolve to be faithful. The gospel portrays both the journey and the reward in terms of blessedness.

✦ My life has been shaped by the Beatitudes in that . . .

Brief Silence

Prayer

Almighty God, you are the source of all blessings. Help us to be faithful to our ministry so that we might be a blessing for others. We ask this through Christ our Lord. **Amen.**

THE COMMEMORATION OF ALL THE FAITHFUL DEPARTED (ALL SOULS)

As we commemorate the faithful departed, it is our abiding hope that the souls of the just are in the hand of God. Let us remember our beloved ones who have died and pray for them . . .

Prayer
Merciful Father, you will that we all share in your eternal life. Help us to be faithful to your will, so that we will one day join our departed loved ones in heaven. We ask this through Christ our Lord. **Amen.**

Gospel (John 6:37-40 [see page 129 for other Gospel options])
Jesus said to the crowds: "Everything that the Father gives me will come to me, and I will not reject anyone who comes to me, because I came down from heaven not to do my own will but the will of the one who sent me. And this is the will of the one who sent me, that I should not lose anything of what he gave me, but that I should raise it on the last day. For this is the will of my Father, that everyone who sees the Son and believes in him may have eternal life, and I shall raise him up on the last day."

Brief Silence

NOVEMBER 2, 2008

For Reflection

The church gathers on this day not to mourn our beloved dead but to give voice to our hope for them and rejoice in their faithfulness. The faithful departed for whom we pray are not enjoying the fullness of heaven; but they have died faithful to their baptismal call to be disciples of Jesus and so neither are they condemned to everlasting punishment.

The gospel twice points to the hope we have for those faithful who have died but have not yet received the fullness of eternal life: Jesus promises that "I will not reject anyone" and "I should not lose anything." The basis for this hope lies in Jesus himself who passed from death to life. It is not easy to move from mourning to hope. The value of annually celebrating this feast day is that we remember our beloved dead in the midst of a community of faith that believes in the hope of the gospel. Having passed through trial and testing, the faithful departed are now graced with peace, understanding, love, and mercy. We are called *now* to live lives of prayer, penance, and good works; we ought not live our faith minimally and hope for the best after we die, relying on God's mercy. God is forgiving and merciful, to be sure, but at the same time we are called to be faithful disciples of Jesus. Surely this is a day of hope!

✦ Jesus' promise for my deceased beloved—"I should not lose anything of what [the Father] gave me"—comforts me because . . .

Brief Silence

Prayer

Loving God, you will that all be united with you in everlasting happiness. Help us to believe in your words of hope and comfort, and to be faithful to your will. We ask this through Christ our Lord. **Amen.**

Other Gospel options for November 2:
Matthew 5:1-12a / Matthew 11:25-30 / Matthew 25:31-46 / Luke 7:11-17 / Luke 23:44-46, 50, 52-53; 24:1-6a / Luke 24:13-16, 28-35 / John 5:24-29 / John 6:51-58 / John 11:17-27 / John 11:32-45 / John 14:1-6

DEDICATION OF THE LATERAN BASILICA IN ROME

We celebrate today the feast of the Dedication of the Lateran Basilica, which is the Pope's cathedral in Rome and our mother church. Let us reflect on the presence of Christ in our midst, and ask that we may become more perfectly what we are—his living temple . . .

Prayer

Heavenly Father, your divine Son was the living temple of your presence. Help us to be that presence for others and to have zeal for prayer and worship. We ask this through Christ our Lord. **Amen.**

Gospel (John 2:13-22)

Since the Passover of the Jews was near, Jesus went up to Jerusalem. He found in the temple area those who sold oxen, sheep, and doves, as well as the money changers seated there. He made a whip out of cords and drove them all out of the temple area, with the sheep and oxen, and spilled the coins of the money changers and overturned their tables, and to those who sold doves he said, "Take these out of here, and stop making my Father's house a marketplace." His disciples recalled the words of Scripture, *Zeal for your house will consume me.* At this the Jews answered and said to him, "What sign can you show us for doing this?" Jesus answered and said to them, "Destroy this temple and in three days I will raise it up." The Jews said, "This temple has been under construction for forty-six years, and you will raise it up in three days?" But he was speaking about the temple of his Body. Therefore, when he was raised from the dead, his disciples remembered that he had said this, and they came to believe the Scripture and the word Jesus had spoken.

Brief Silence

NOVEMBER 9, 2008

For Reflection

This feast day celebrates an important building, which is a symbol for Western Christendom. The Lateran Basilica is important not because of its brick and mortar, not because it is a symbol invoking in us powerful responses, but because it represents our common identity as church, as the Body of Christ. Both the readings and the meaning of this feast remind us that we celebrate not simply a building but the living reality of the church. Just as the Temple in Jerusalem was a symbol of identity for Israel (see the gospel), so is the Lateran Basilica a symbol of identity for us, the church.

This gospel episode takes place near Passover (the major feast of Israel's identity) and at the Temple (the major symbol of this identity). When Jesus speaks of his body as temple, he transfers the symbol of identity from the Temple in Jerusalem to himself. Building upon this understanding, St. Paul in the second reading identifies the community of believers as "the temple of God" and the dwelling place of the Spirit. As we commemorate the dedication of the Lateran Basilica, we celebrate this church building as a symbol of our deepest identity: we are the living temple of God and the Body of Christ.

✦ The implication for me of this feast expanding the temple symbol to include God's people is . . .

Brief Silence

Prayer

Gracious God, you built your church upon Christ Jesus as its cornerstone. Help us to turn to this Rock of our salvation in times of need, and to be faithful to being the living temple of his Body. We ask this through Christ our Lord. **Amen.**

THIRTY-THIRD SUNDAY IN ORDINARY TIME

Let us reflect on how faithful we have been in even the small matters of living the life of a disciple . . .

Prayer
O God, you have entrusted to us the continuation of your Son's work of salvation. Strengthen us for this awesome and wondrous task. We ask this through Christ our Lord. **Amen.**

Gospel (Matt 25:14-15, 19-21 [Longer Form: Matt 25:14-30])
Jesus told his disciples this parable: "A man going on a journey called in his servants and entrusted his possessions to them. To one he gave five talents; to another, two; to a third, one—to each according to his ability. Then he went away.

"After a long time the master of those servants came back and settled accounts with them. The one who had received five talents came forward bringing the additional five. He said, 'Master, you gave me five talents. See, I have made five more.' His master said to him, 'Well done, my good and faithful servant. Since you were faithful in small matters, I will give you great responsibilities. Come, share your master's joy.'"

Brief Silence

For Reflection

The servant who received one talent dug a hole and buried it. In the culture of biblical times, burying the talent was actually quite prudent; had the talent been lost he would not have been accountable to his master because he was not careless in taking care of the master's property. Culpability was only exacted when one was careless. This servant was prudent, safe; but he took no risks.

In our own gospel living we can be prudent and safe. We can do what is necessary—go to Mass, get to confession, say our daily prayers—but take no risks. Real growth in gospel living comes in taking risks. We risk dying when we see a stranger who is poor and in need, and we reach out to him or her. We risk dying when we share our own talents by volunteering for a liturgical ministry or for one of the parish committees, even if we feel others may be more qualified. We risk dying by sharing our abundance with others who are less fortunate. Always, though, when we risk dying to self, we receive from God an abundance of life, because in the dying to self we are more perfectly conformed to Christ. The shock of this gospel is the extravagance of what is being given us. All we need do is be faithful in "small matters." Then we, indeed, will "share in [our] master's joy."

✦ The "richness" that I have received while remaining faithful to the small matters in my ministry and discipleship is . . .

Brief Silence

Prayer

God of salvation, you have enriched us with every good thing. Help us to be faithful in all you ask of us and come to our eternal reward. We ask this through Christ our Lord.
Amen.

THE SOLEMNITY OF OUR LORD JESUS CHRIST THE KING

This solemnity of Our Lord Jesus Christ the King celebrates his victory over death and his eternal glory. Let us prepare well to worship and acclaim our victorious Lord . . .

Prayer

God of power and might, you judge us justly and desire that we share in your eternal life. Help us to reach out to the Christ in others, so that we might prepare ourselves well for the glory that awaits those who are faithful. We ask this through Christ our Lord. **Amen**.

Gospel (Matt 25:31-46)

Jesus said to his disciples: "When the Son of Man comes in his glory, and all the angels with him, he will sit upon his glorious throne, and all the nations will be assembled before him. And he will separate them one from another, as a shepherd separates the sheep from the goats. He will place the sheep on his right and the goats on his left. Then the king will say to those on his right, 'Come, you who are blessed by my Father. Inherit the kingdom prepared for you from the foundation of the world. For I was hungry and you gave me food, I was thirsty and you gave me drink, a stranger and you welcomed me, naked and you clothed me, ill and you cared for me, in prison and you visited me.' Then the righteous will answer him and say, 'Lord, when did we see you hungry and feed you, or thirsty and give you drink? When did we see you a stranger and welcome you, or naked and clothe you? When did we see you ill or in prison, and visit you?" And the king will say to them in reply, 'Amen, I say to you, whatever you did for one of the least brothers of mine, you did for me.' Then he will say to those on his left, 'Depart from me, you accursed, into the eternal fire prepared for the devil and his angels. For I was hungry and you gave me no food, I was thirsty and you gave me no drink, a stranger and you gave me no welcome, naked and you gave me no clothing, ill and in prison, and you did not care for me.' Then they will answer and say, 'Lord, when did we see you hungry or thirsty or a stranger or naked or ill or in prison, and not minister to your needs?' He will answer them, 'Amen, I say to you, what you did not do for one of these least ones, you did not do for me.' And these will go off to eternal punishment, but the righteous to eternal life."

Brief Silence

For Reflection

This solemnity celebrates the victory and glory of Christ. The gospel gives a clear blueprint for how we ourselves might share in that glory: do good to the least among us. Christ's judgment, "Come" or "Depart," should be no surprise because we have, by our actions, said the same to the needy throughout our lives. Our conduct during this life is, in fact, our choice of the words we hear Jesus say to us at our final judgment. Our choices now are already our choice for eternity.

Christ exercises his sovereignty (kingship) in the right to judge. The basis for his judgment of us is whether we care for the least among us. What's surprising about the judgment is that neither the good nor the wicked knew that what they were doing or not doing was for Christ. Christ is not a vindictive judge; we are judged only on our own choices and actions. The graciousness of Christ, the "Son of Man [who] comes in his glory," is that this solemnity isn't just about his victory and glory. By inviting us to share in this eschatological glory we are celebrating our own victory as well. Such is the Sovereign King we have!

✦ The bases for whether I help another or not are . . . The limits to my care and concern for others are . . .

Brief Silence

Prayer

Gracious God, you invite us to inherit the eternal life prepared for us by your Son's death and resurrection. Strengthen us on our life's journey and help us to be kind and generous to others who bear the face of our Lord and Savior Jesus Christ. We ask this through Christ our Lord. **Amen.**